Bomber Bases of
World War 2
1st Air Division
8th Air Force USAAF
1942–45

Bomber Bases of World War 2 1st Air Division 8th Air Force USAAF 1942–45

Flying Fortress Squadrons in
Cambridgeshire, Bedfordshire,
Huntingdonshire, Essex, Hertfordshire
and Northamptonshire

Martin W. Bowman

Pen & Sword
AVIATION

First published in Great Britain in 2007 by
Pen & Sword Aviation
an imprint of
Pen & Sword Books Ltd

Copyright © Martin W. Bowman, 2007

ISBN 978 1 84415 453 1

A CIP catalogue record for this book is
available from the British Library

Typeset in Palatino by
Phoenix Typesetting, Auldgirth, Dumfriesshire

Printed and bound in England by
CPI UK

Pen & Sword Books Ltd incorporates the Imprints of Pen & Sword Aviation,
Pen & Sword Maritime, Pen & Sword Military, Wharncliffe Local History,
Pen & Sword Select, Pen & Sword Military Classics and Leo Cooper.

For a complete list of Pen & Sword titles please contact
PEN & SWORD BOOKS LIMITED
47 Church Street, Barnsley, South Yorkshire, S70 2AS, England
E-mail: enquiries@pen-and-sword.co.uk
Website: www.pen-and-sword.co.uk

Contents

Acknowledgements

Bedford Tourist Information Centre; Ken Blakeborough; Bill Donald; East Northamptonshire Council; 8th Air Force Historical Society; Mike Fuenfer; GMS Enterprises; Larry Goldstein; Steve Gotts; Howard E. Hernan; Imperial War Museum, Duxford; Dick Johnson; General Lewis E. Lyle; Ron MacKay; the late Brian S. McGuire; Joseph Minton; the Northamptonshire Enterprise Agency; Maurice 'Mo' A. Preston; Cliff Pyle; Connie and Gordon Richards, Ben Smith Jnr.; Paul Tibbets; William C. Stewart; Pete Worby; Joe Wroblewski.

The 8th Air Force Bombing Offensive 1942–5

Before the USA's entry into World War II, brought about by the Japanese attack on Pearl Harbor on 7 December 1941, far-reaching decisions had been made in the event that the USA should become involved in the conflict with the Axis powers. Between 27 January and 27 March 1941 agreements between the US and Great Britain were made for the provision of naval, ground and air support for the campaign against Germany. As a result, a special US Army Observer Group, headed by Major General James F. Chaney, was activated in London on 19 May 1941. One of Chaney's first tasks was to reconnoitre areas regarded as potential sites for US Army Air Force (USAAF) installations. During late 1941 several tentative sites were explored, including Prestwick near Ayr in Scotland and Warton near Liverpool, the proposed site for a repair depot. Others, like Polebrook, Grafton Underwood, Kimbolton, Molesworth, Chelveston, Podington and Thurleigh, all in the Huntingdon area, would soon become familiar bases of B-17 Flying Fortress groups of the 8th Air Force Bomber Command.

On 2 January 1942 the order activating the 8th Air Force was signed by Major General Henry 'Hap' Arnold, the Commanding General, Army Air Forces, and the headquarters was formed at

Savannah, Georgia, twenty-six days later. On 8 January it was announced that a bomber command was to be established in England. Arnold designated General Ira C. Eaker as Commanding General of VIII Bomber Command and his duties were to help prepare airfields and installations and understudy the methods of RAF Bomber Command. Initially, Eaker's headquarters was established at RAF Bomber Command HQ, High Wycombe, Buckinghamshire. It was here, on 22 February, that VIII Bomber Command was formally activated. Almost six months were to elapse before the 8th Air Force mounted its first all-American bombing mission on German-held territory. Between 31 March and 3 April 1942 Eaker and his staff officers made a more detailed reconnaissance of the Huntingdon area and the seeds of the future American presence were thus sown.

The Air Ministry and American Engineer battalions cut a swathe through the furrowed fields of East Anglia, leaving in their wake bases destined for use by bomb wings and fighter groups. At first the USAAF had only seventy-five airfields in the United Kingdom, but the total eventually reached 250, costing

GIs helping with the harvest near Thurleigh in 1943. *(Richards)*

£645 million, £40 million of which was found by the American Government. By the end of World War II, 360,000 acres of land had been occupied by airfields and a staggering 160 million square yards of concrete and tarmac had been laid down. The Class A type airfield consisted of three intersecting runways, with the main runway aligned to the prevailing wind, being 2000 yards long and the other two 1400 yards long. Each runway was standardised at fifty yards wide and a 50-foot wide perimeter track or taxiway encircled the runway and joined the end of each. Branching off the taxiways were fifty hardstands and dispersal points for the bombers. The type of hangar varied but the T2, a rectangular, steel-framed 240-foot long building, 39 feet high and 120 feet span, clad with corrugated steel sheet and with sliding doors at each end, was the most numerous. The total number of personnel on a base was approximately 2500 men. Passing vehicles showered the men with mud as they walked and cycled from their Nissen huts to the mess halls and briefing rooms before take-off. In winter, interminable rain and fog so thick you had to cut it before you could walk made life unbearable.

Bill Ong, a US Army engineer who helped build airfields recalls:

Training in the sunshine of Texas is one thing. Building airfields in the desert was easy – in East Anglia it was sure something else . . . . We weren't really popular with the local population. They didn't take kindly to us Americans moving in and tearing up their countryside. I tell you, what with the weather, the cold, the mud – well, fighting the Germans would have been child's play compared to all this. But we didn't blame the people for feeling the way they did. They knew that we were there to ruin their land – and when we had ruined it would then fly hundreds of aeroplanes from this base and low over their homes. . . . The completed airfield would house maybe three or four squadrons of B-17s and include bomb storage sites, petrol dumps, airfield lighting, water towers, fire stations – not to mention landscaping, outside painting, interior decoration and a whole host of jobs too numerous to mention. There would eventually be 500 buildings of several different types. They would of course be widely dispersed across and around the field. Living quarters and admin buildings were mostly of the Nissen type and there were also the larger Romsey-type huts. The control tower and the parachute stores were built of brick. Apart from the headquarters building, these were the only ones on the site that could be considered permanent structures. This was something to do with the land that we were building on – it had been requisitioned by the British Air Ministry and the Government had promised the owners that as soon as the war was over the land would be returned to agricultural use. Hogwash! We knew it would take years to reconstitute the land after the war, if it could ever be rescued properly at all. But that wasn't our problem.

Meanwhile, in America, B-17 and B-24 heavy bombardment groups were activated for deployment to Britain. The first of the B-17 groups activated was the 34th, at Langley Field, Virginia, on 15 January 1942, but the Group was used to train other groups and remained in America until late March 1944. From February to March 1942 four more B-17 groups, the 97th, 301st, 303rd and the 92nd, were formally activated. It fell to these three groups and two Liberator units, to establish the nucleus of the 8th Air Force's heavy bombardment force in England. In August the 1st Bomb Wing was activated to embrace all the B-17 groups in the western part of East Anglia, while the 4th Wing controlled the B-17 groups in Suffolk and Essex. By the end of August 1942 over 100 B-17s, enough for three groups, had arrived in the UK. On 17 August, the 8th Air Force flew its first mission of the war when several Fortresses were dispatched to north-eastern France, where they bombed a large marshalling yard. B-17 crews threw themselves headlong into a bitter war over Europe in daylight and without escort, despite opposition, particularly from the US Navy, which was convinced that America's first objective lay in the defeat of Japan. American and RAF air leaders disagreed on the best method for employing strategic air forces against Germany. The British wanted the 8th Air Force to join RAF Bomber Command in its night bombing offensive, but

The crew of B-17F 41-24444 *The Red Gremlin* in the 340th Bomb Squadron, 97th Bomb Group, pose for a Group photograph on 9 September 1942. In the back row, far left, is Major Paul W. Tibbets. On 17 August 1942 Tibbets and his CO, Colonel Frank A. Armstrong Jr, led the first Fortress raid from England in *Butcher Shop*. Three years later, on 6 August 1945, Tibbets, his bombardier Tom Ferebee (back row, third from left) and navigator 'Dutch' Van Kirk (back row, third from right), flew in the same positions in B-29 *Enola Gay* on the first atomic bomb drop, on Hiroshima, Japan. *(Paul Tibbets Collection)*

the USAAF was determined to pursue its daylight precision bombing strategy.

On 5 September 1942 the 301st Bomb Group flew its first mission and on 6 September the largest bombing mission so far took place when thirty-six B-17s raided the Avions Potez factory at Méaulte. Further missions followed, to the Rotterdam shipyards, Cherbourg and to Méaulte and St Omer/Longuenesse airfield. On 9 October, eighty-four B-17s, including twenty-four from the 306th Bomb Group based at Thurleigh, Bedfordshire, went to the huge steel and locomotive works at Lille. Six B-17s were shot down by fighters. Only sixty-nine bombers hit their primary targets and many of the bombs failed to explode. Many bombs fell outside the target area, killing a number of French civilians.

On 20 October 1942 Brigadier General Asa N. Duncan, Chief of the Air Staff, issued a revised set of objectives to be carried out by VIII Bomber Command. In part, it stated '. . . Until further orders, every effort of the VIIIth Bomber Command will be directed to obtaining the maximum destruction of the submarine bases in the Bay of Biscay . . .' Losses were high and results poor. On 7 November the 91st Bomb Group flew its first mission when sixty-eight B-17s and B-24s went to the U-boat pens at Brest. On 18 November the 303rd Bomb Group flew its first mission. On 22 November Colonel Curtis E. LeMay's 305th Bomb Group flew its inaugural mission, part of a force of sixty-eight B-17s and eight Liberators, to Lorient. LeMay was determined to improve bombing accuracy and insisted his crews flew a straight course on the bomb run instead of zigzagging every ten seconds, a tactic that had been designed to spoil the aim of the German flak batteries. He tried this formation for the first time on 23 November, when VIII Bomber Command went to St Nazaire again. Bad weather and mechanical problems forced several bombers to abort, but LeMay's tactics worked and none in the 305th Bomb Group were lost. Other groups suffered, however. The *Luftwaffe* had revised its tactics too, concentrating its attacks on the frontal area of a B-17 where the defensive fire-power was weakest. In one pass, fighters knocked down four B-17s and a fifth victim staggered home to crash in England. Small-scale raids continued against the U-boat pens and airfields in France. By the year-end, formations of eighty-plus Fortresses became usual.

Early in January 1943 Eaker abandoned individual bombing, which had been SOP (Standard Operating Procedure), in favour of group bombing, because 'lead crews' and 'staggered forma-tions', developed by Colonel LeMay, proved more effective. However, losses reached a new high. The growing strength of VIII Bomber Command increased pressure on the *Luftwaffe*, which now attacked in larger formations, and simultaneous attacks by fighters, rather than in trail, were used. Attacks from 12 o'clock high became the norm.

On 27 January 1943, VIII Bomber Command attacked

Germany for the first time when fifty-five Fortresses reached
Wilhelmshaven. During February and March 1943 aircraft
factories, U-boat bases and marshalling yards were bombed. On
8 March P-47C Thunderbolt fighters escorted the bombers for
the first time. With escorts and rising bomber strengths, on 18
March seventy-three Fortresses and twenty-four Liberators, the
highest number of bombers so far, attacked shipbuilding yards a
few miles north of Bremen and on 22 March eighty-four
Liberators and Fortresses attacked U-boat yards at Wilhelmshaven. Missions were flown almost daily. On 31 March, 102
B-17s and B-24s were dispatched to bomb the dock area at
Rotterdam, but four bomb groups were recalled because of
strong winds and thick cloud. Two 303rd Bomb Group B-17s
were lost in a mid-air collision. Thirty-three bombers hit the
dock area but many heavies, blown off course by strong winds
and bad visibility, missed their objectives completely and killed
326 Dutch civilians when their bombs exploded in the streets of
Rotterdam.

During April 1943 attacks were made on industrial targets in
France and Belgium. On 17 April, a record 111 bombers bombed
the Focke-Wulf factory at Bremen. Intense fighter attacks shot
down fifteen Fortresses, and thirty-nine more suffered battle
damage. During May 1943 attacks were made on U-boat pens,
and industrial targets in France and Belgium. On 14 May the 8th
Air Force made simultaneous attacks on four targets, but the
day's missions cost twelve B-17s and B-24s. Sixty-seven fighters
were claimed shot down. In June 1943 multiple attacks on a
given day continued. Eaker was able to send the 1st and 4th
Bomb Wings on two-pronged attacks against north German
targets at Emden, Kiel, Bremen, Wilhelmshaven and Cuxhaven
on a single day. On 11 June when the B-17s set out to bomb
Bremen, the 1st Bomb Wing lost eight B-17s and sixty-two
Fortresses returned damaged. The American gunners claimed to
have shot down eighty-five enemy fighters. In fact, only seven
German fighters were destroyed or damaged and two pilots
were injured. On 22 June the 8th Air Force made its first large-
scale attack on the Ruhr, when 182 heavies bombed the chemical
and synthetic rubber plant at Hüls. Two new 1st Bomb Wing
groups, the 381st and 384th, flew their first mission this day.

Sixteen B-17s were shot down. Despite continuing losses, the addition of more groups allowed Eaker to send a record 322 bombers to Hannover on 17 July. On 24 July a weeklong series of heavy bomber raids, later called 'Blitz Week', went ahead, beginning with a raid by 208 B-17s on Heroya and Trondheim in Norway. One B-17 failed to return and sixty-four were battle-damaged. The next day, 25 July, 218 bombers attacked Hamburg, devastated the night before in the great RAF Bomber Command fire raid, and Kiel. Cloud cover and the huge smoke pall from the still burning fires at Hamburg caused fifty-nine B-17s of the 92nd, 305th and 306th Bomb Groups to abandon their strike altogether. The Hamburg force was intercepted as the leading B-17s approached the Elbe estuary. In running battles, fifteen B-17s – seven of them from the 384th Bomb Group – were shot down, and sixty-seven returned battle-damaged. The Kiel force lost four B-17s and fifty returned damaged, two of which crashed on landing.

On 26 July ninety-two heavies bombed rubber factories at Hannover and fifty-four others attacked shipbuilding yards at Hamburg. Twenty-four aircraft were lost, mostly to enemy fighters. After a stand down on 27 July, the 8th Air Force dispatched just over 300 bombers on 28 July in two forces to bomb German targets. However, bad weather affected the mission and only forty-nine bombed the Fieseler aircraft works at Kassel, with twenty-eight hitting the Fw 190 factory at Oschersleben. Twenty-two bombers were lost. On 29 July 168 B-17s of the 1st Bomb Wing were dispatched to bomb the U-boat yards at Kiel. The 1st Bomb Wing lost six B-17s, four of them from the 306th Bomb Group. On 30 July 186 B-17s went to Kassel. Altogether, twelve bombers and six US fighters were lost. The next day, 31 July, VIII Bomber Command announced a three-day stand down from combat. In a week of sustained operations, about 100 aircraft and ninety combat crews had been lost.

On 12 August 243 unescorted heavy bombers were dispatched to targets in the Ruhr. Some twenty-five bombers were shot down. Over 300 bombers were sent to attack targets in Holland and France on 15 August. This was part of the *Starkey* deception plan, which was created to make the Germans believe that an invasion of the French coast was imminent, to relieve some of the pressure on Russia and halt troop movements to Italy. Strikes against enemy airfields in France and the Low Countries continued on 16 August, then early that evening base operation staff throughout eastern England waited for their orders for the morrow; the anniversary mission of the 8th Air Force. Eaker and his planners had conceived a most ambitious and daring plan to attack aircraft plants at Schweinfurt and Regensburg simultaneously. Colonel Curtis E. LeMay led the 4th Bomb Wing to Regensburg. To minimise attacks from enemy fighters, it was decided that LeMay's B-17s would fly on to North Africa after the target. Brigadier General Robert Williams, CO, 1st Bomb Wing, meanwhile, would lead his force on a parallel course to Schweinfurt further to confuse the enemy defences and return to England after the raid. (Not enough 1st Bomb Wing Fortresses were equipped with 'Tokyo tanks' and could not make the 725-mile trip). Unfortunately, the 1st Bomb Wing was delayed by thick inland mists for three and a half hours after the 4th Bomb Wing had taken off and this effectively prevented a two-pronged assault that might have split the opposing fighter force. The delay gave the *Luftwaffe* time to refuel, rearm, and redeploy to forward bases in Holland after dealing with the Regensburg force. Despite a strong fighter escort, the 4th Bomb Wing lost twenty-four B-17s and the Schweinfurt force lost thirty-six Fortresses. Worst hit were the 381st and 91st Bomb Groups, which lost eleven and ten B-17s respectively. Twenty-seven B-17s in the 1st Bomb Wing were so badly damaged that they never flew again and sixty Fortresses had to be left in North Africa pending repairs, so in the final analysis, 147 Fortresses had been lost to all causes. The *Luftwaffe* lost twenty-seven fighters, as against claims by the B-17 gunners and escorting fighters of 288 German fighters destroyed!

For a time the Schweinfurt losses had a significant effect on the B-17 groups but the P-47D, with the installation of a 108-gallon belly tank, could now escort the bombers further. *Carpet* radar jammers on B-17s also helped confuse enemy radar. However, despite round-the-clock bombing of aircraft production plants, the *Luftwaffe* had a first-line strength of 1525 single and twin-engined fighters for the defence of the western approaches to Germany. In reality, the *Luftwaffe* had 1646 single and twin-engined fighters, 400 more than before the issue of the *Pointblank* directive, although only about a third of this force was ready for immediate use, the remainder being reserves or temporarily unserviceable. Early in October, therefore, the decision was taken to attack the ball bearing plant at Schweinfurt for the second time in three months to deliver a single, decisive blow against the German aircraft industry and stem the flow of fighters to the *Luftwaffe*. The mission went ahead on 14 October, but the hoped for force of 420 Fortresses and Liberators in a three-pronged attack was defeated by bad weather and aborts. Ultimately, 320 B-17s were dispatched. Schweinfurt soaked up 482.8 tons of high explosives and incendiaries but American losses were high. The 1st Bomb Division (in September the 1st, 2nd and 4th Bomb Wings were renumbered as 1st, 2nd and 3rd Bomb Divisions) lost forty-five B-17s and the 3rd Bomb Division lost fifteen Fortresses. Sixty Fortresses and 600 men were missing. Five B-17s had crashed in England as a result of their battle-damaged condition and twelve more were destroyed in crash-landings or so badly damaged that they had to be written off. Of the returning bombers, 121 required repairs. Claims of 186 enemy fighters shot down were submitted (the true figure was about thirty-five). Only eighty-eight out of the 1222 bombs dropped actually fell on the plants and production at the Kugelfischer plant, largest of the five plants, was interrupted for only six weeks.

The losses and a spell of bad weather restricted VIII Bomber Command to just two more missions in October. After the Schweinfurt mission, desperate attempts were made to improve the range of the few Thunderbolts in the European Theater of Operations (ETO). Still, the long-range missions persisted. On 3 November 566 B-17s and B-24s were dispatched to Wilhelmshaven. Seven bombers were lost in a fierce air battle. Two days later 323 B-17s bombed Gelsenkirchen and 104 B-24s hit Munster. Eight B-17s were lost. For the first two weeks of November 1943, England was blanketed by thick fog and airfields were lashed with intermittent showers and high winds. When the bad weather front finally lifted on 16 November, VIII Bomber Command struck at targets in Norway. The 1st Bomb

Division attacked the molybdenum mines at Knaben and the 3rd Bomb Division attacked a generating plant at Vermark in the Rjukan Valley. Both targets were connected with the German heavy water experiments, which were designed to give the Nazis the atomic bomb. On 31 December, when VIII Bomber Command completed its second year in England with all-out raids on airfields in France, twenty-five bomber crews and four fighter pilots would not return to their bases to celebrate New Year's Eve.

Early in 1944 the *Luftwaffe* was still a force to be reckoned with, but long-range P-51 Mustangs could accompany the bombers to their targets and back again. General Carl 'Tooey' Spaatz and his subordinate commanders, Major General Jimmy Doolittle (8th Air Force) and Major General Nathan F. Twining (15th Air Force), planned to make a series of co-ordinated raids on the German aircraft industry, supported by RAF night bombing, at the earliest possible date. Good weather finally permitted Operation *Argument*, which soon became known as 'Big Week', to take place during the week 20–25 February. On 20 February 1028 B-17s and B-24s and 832 fighters in the 8th Air Force attacked twelve aircraft plants in Germany for the loss of twenty-five bombers and four fighters. Three Medals of Honor (two posthumously) were awarded to 1st Bomb Division B-17 airmen. The next day, 21 February, 924 bombers and 679 fighters bombed aircraft factories at Brunswick and other targets. The 8th Air Force lost nineteen bombers and five fighters, but sixty German fighters were claimed shot down. On 22 February the 8th Air Force bombed targets in Germany and Holland with the loss of forty-one bombers. On 23 February bad weather kept the heavies on the ground. The next day, 24 February, 238 Fortresses attacked Schweinfurt, losing eleven B-17s, while 295 B-17s struck at targets on the Baltic coast with the loss of five Fortresses. On 25 February the USSTAF brought the curtain down on 'Big Week' when 1300 8th and 15th Air Force bombers and 1000 fighters were dispatched to aircraft plants, ball bearing works and components factories throughout the Reich. The 1st Bomb Division caused heavy damage to the Messerschmitt plants at Augsburg and the ball bearing plants at Stuttgart were also bombed. Output at both Augsburg and Regensburg was severely reduced for four months following the raids. The 8th Air Force lost thirty-one bombers. In all, 'Big Week' cost 226 bombers.

Less than a week later, the 8th Air Force bombed 'Big B' – Berlin – for the first time. An attack on 3 March was aborted because of bad weather and the next day it prevented all except 502 Fortresses and 770 fighters from continuing to the target before severe weather *en route* resulted in a recall. Thirty 3rd Bomb Division B-17s dropped the first American bombs on the German capital. On 6 March the 8th Air Force dispatched 730 B-17s and B-24s and 801 escort fighters to targets in the suburbs of Berlin. US fighters claimed eighty-one enemy fighters shot down and the bomber gunners claimed ninety-seven destroyed (the *Luftwaffe* actually lost sixty-four fighters destroyed). The 8th Air Force lost a record sixty-nine bombers and eleven fighters, while 102 bombers were seriously damaged. Groups were stood down on 7 March before they resumed the daylight offensive against Berlin again on 8 March. A total of 623 bombers were sent to bomb the VKF ball-bearing plant at Erkner in the suburbs of Berlin, escorted by 891 fighters. Of the force, 539 heavies got their bombs away over the German capital, which once again was heavily defended. The leading 3rd Bomb Division lost twenty-three Fortresses and the 1st Bomb Division lost five B-17s to fighter attacks and flak. Nine B-24s and eighteen fighters were lost. The heavy bomber gunners claimed to have shot down sixty-three enemy fighters, while the escorts claimed a further seventy-nine for the loss of eighteen of their own. In fact, only twenty-seven *Luftwaffe* fighters were lost on 8 March. Despite the continued high losses, the 8th Air Force attacked Berlin again on 9 March. A total of 361 B-17s bombed Big B, while 165 Liberators visited Hannover, Brunswick and Nienburg. Weather conditions kept the enemy fighters on the ground and the 800 escort fighters returned without claiming any enemy fighters. The B-17 groups lost six of their number over Berlin to flak.

Smaller-scale raids on targets in France and Germany followed. On 13 April 1944 overall command of the Combined Bomber Offensive and the 8th Air Force officially passed to General Dwight D. Eisenhower, newly appointed Supreme Allied Commander. Missions in April and May alternated between targets in Germany and hitting targets in France,

Luxembourg and Belgium. Operation *Cover* called for raids on coastal defences, mainly in the Pas de Calais, to deceive the Germans as to the area to be invaded by the Allied armies massing in Britain. On 6 June 1944, *D-Day*, a total of 2362 bomber sorties, involving 1729 B-17s and B-24s, was flown, dropping 3596 tons of bombs. US ground crews worked throughout the night of 6 June and all day on 7 June so that two missions could be flown. On 8 June 1135 bombers were dispatched to communication targets in France. Bad weather prevented 400 heavies from bombing, and the next day postponed any bomber strikes at all. It also severely curtailed operations on 10 June. Of the 873 bombers airborne, over 200 were forced to abort because of cloud conditions. Some 589 bombers, including thirty-one Pathfinders, attacked eight airfields in France and nine coastal installations in the Pas de Calais. On 11 and 12 June bad weather ruled out targets in Germany and the 8th Air Force dispatched its bombers to France again. Tactical targets in France continued to be attacked until 15 June, when 1225 bombers attacked an oil refinery at Misburg, and the 1st Bomb Division struck mostly at airfield targets in northern France, which could be used to launch *Luftwaffe* attacks on the Normandy bridgehead.

From June onwards, mass formations of over a thousand bombers were not uncommon as the 8th Air Force carried out post invasion support missions and bombed targets throughout the Reich. It seemed that the war would be over by Christmas. However, on 16 December 1944, using appalling weather conditions to his advantage, Field Marshal Karl von Rundstedt and his panzer formations attacked American positions in the forests of the Ardennes on the French-Belgian border. They opened up a salient or 'bulge' in the Allied lines, supported by an estimated 1400 German fighters. The Allied air forces were grounded by fog and it was not until 23 December that they could offer bomber support in the 'Battle of the Bulge'. On Christmas Eve a record 2034 8th Air Force bombers and 500 RAF and 9th Air Force bombers, took part in the largest single strike flown by the Allied Air Forces in World War II, against German airfields and lines of communication leading to the 'Bulge'. Overall, the Christmas Eve raids were effective and severely hampered von Rundstedt's lines of communication.

German production of fighter aircraft actually increased through 1944 into 1945. It had peaked in September 1944, when an astonishing 1874 Bf 109s and 1002 Fw 190s were completed. The USSTAF was clearly winning the battle of attrition. January 1945 marked the 8th Air Force's third year of operations and it seemed as if the end of the war was in sight. Finally, the German advance in the Ardennes came to a halt and ultimately petered out. Hitler's last chance now lay in his so-called 'wonder weapons' – the V1 and V2. Missions were flown to tactical targets throughout the remaining days of January, but when the weather intervened, the 8th Air Force mounted shallow penetration raids on *Noball* targets in France. The 8th Air Force also attempted several tactical missions, but the weather was so bad morale sagged as mission after mission was scrubbed, often just after take-off.

By 3 February 1945 the Red Army was only 35 miles from Berlin and the capital was jammed with refugees fleeing from the advancing Russians. Accompanied by 900 fighters, 1200 B-17s and B-24s dropped 2267 tons of bombs on the centre of Berlin, killing an estimated 25,000 inhabitants and destroying 360 industrial firms, heavily damaging another 170. The 8th Air Force lost twenty-one bombers shot down and another six crash-landed inside the Russian lines. Of the bombers that returned, ninety-three had suffered varying forms of major flak damage. On 9 February the heavies returned to the oil refineries in the ever-diminishing Reich. On 22 February *Clarion,* the systematic destruction of the German communications network, was launched. More than 6000 Allied aircraft struck at transportation targets throughout western Germany and northern Holland. Only seven bombers, including two B-17s, were lost. By March 1945 the systematic destruction of German oil production plants had virtually driven the *Luftwaffe* from German skies, although Me 262 jet fighters could still be expected to put in rare attacks. On 23/24 March, under a 66-mile long smokescreen and aided by 1749 bombers of the 8th Air Force, Field Marshal Bernard Montgomery's 21st Army Group crossed the Rhine in the north, while further south simultaneous crossings were made by General Patton's Third Army.

Beginning on 5 April, the weather over the continent

improved dramatically and the B-17s were dispatched to U-boat pens on the Baltic coast. Everywhere the Allies were victorious. In Germany, last-ditch attempts were made by the *Luftwaffe* to try to stem the tide and even the deliberate ramming of American bombers by converted Bf 109 fighters, called *Rammjäger*, was tried. They could not prevent the final outcome, however. During the week 18 to 25 April, 8th Air Force missions were briefed and scrubbed almost simultaneously as the ground forces overran objective after objective. The end came on 25 April 1945 when 306 B-17s of the 1st Air Division bombed the Skoda armaments factory at Pilsen in Czechoslovakia. During the first week of May the German armies surrendered and in the same month Fortress crews flew mercy missions, called *Chowhound*, to starving Dutch civilians in Holland. VE (Victory in Europe) Day took place on 8 May.

The Airfields

. . . he walked through the winding old streets of Archbury direct to a pub called the Black Swan, borrowed a bicycle from the bartender, slung his package to the handlebars and pedaled out of the village along a country road lined with hedges and shaggy houses with thatched roofs. Presently he turned off on a side road, propped his bike against a hedge and strode slowly a hundred yards out onto an enormous flat, unobstructed field. When he halted he was standing at the head of a wide, dilapidated avenue of concrete, which stretched in front of him with gentle undulations for a mile and a half. A herd of cows, nibbling at the tall grass, which had grown up through the cracks, helped to camouflage his recollection of the huge runway. He noted the black streaks left by tyres, where they had struck the surface, smoking, and nearby, through the weeds which nearly covered it, he could still see the stains left by puddles of grease and black oil on one of the hardstands evenly spaced around the five-mile circumference of the perimeter track, like teeth on a ring gear. And in the background he could make out a forlorn dark green control tower, surmounted by a tattered gray windsock and behind it two empty hangars, a shoe box of a water tank on high stilts and an ugly cluster of squat Nissen huts. Not a soul was visible, nothing moved save the cows, nor was there any sound to break the great quiet. A gust of wind blew back the tall weeds behind the hardstand nearest him. But suddenly Stovall could no longer see the bent-back weeds through the quick tears that blurred his eyes

and slid down the deep lines in his face. He made no move to brush them away. For behind the blur he could see, from within, more clearly. On each empty hardstand there sat the ghost of a B-17, its four whirling propellers blasting the tall grass with the gale of its slip stream, its tires bulging under the weight of tons of bombs and tons of the gasoline needed for a deep penetration.

Twelve O'Clock High by Beirne Lay, Jr and Sy Bartlett

Alconbury (Station 102), Huntingdonshire, now Cambridgeshire

Alconbury opened in 1939 as a satellite airfield for RAF Wyton and was an RAF Blenheim and Wellington station until 1942, when W. & C. French Ltd was contracted to enlarge the airfield for use by American bombers. The main runway was extended from 1375 yards to 2000 yards and two others from 1240 and 1100 yards to 1400 yards. Twenty-six hardstandings were also added to take the total number to fifty and the taxiways were altered. Two T2-type hangars were also constructed on the west and north sides of the airfield. Communal buildings and barrack sites were built in dispersed sites in farmland to the south-west of the airfield on the opposite side of the A14 with accommodation for 421 officers and 2473 men. Bomb and ammunition stores and two underground petrol storage facilities were also built.

In early September 1942 the 93rd Bomb Group arrived from America with B-24D Liberator bombers, which stayed for four months before moving to Hardwick, Norfolk. His Majesty King George VI made his first visit to an 8th Air Force base when he

Alconbury airfield in 1944. *(USAF)*

was shown around Alconbury on 14 November. On 4 January 1943 the 92nd Bomb Group, which had been acting as a B-17 combat crew training and replacement centre at Bovingdon, began arriving at Alconbury minus some of its key personnel and one entire squadron – the 326th. At this time, construction at Alconbury was still in its initial stages. One of the two hangars still had no walls erected and the other was 'an immense bird cage of bare girders'. Few hardstands had been completed and the airfield was a sea of mud. Accommodation was in a poor state and the 325th Squadron area in a shallow valley became known as 'Skunk Hollow'. All flying officers lived in a large estate three miles from the airfield at Upton House and within a few weeks senior officers moved to requisitioned quarters at palatial Stukeley Hall. From 15 April to 15 June 1943 the air echelon of the 95th Bomb Group was based at Alconbury for combat training and the base became very crowded. Their sojourn was marred by a huge explosion on 27 May. A 500-1b bomb detonated and set off several others as ground personnel were bombing up B-17 42-29685 in the dispersal area. Nineteen men died and twenty were severely injured, while four B-17s were destroyed and eleven others were badly damaged.

During May 1943 the 92nd Bomb Group received a dozen YB-40 (B-17) gunships armed with sixteen machine-guns (and an extra top turret and 12,400 rounds of ammunition) and on 14 May the Group flew its first 1943 combat mission. The losses of YB-40s were not made good, although they continued flying missions until the end of July 1943.

On 26 July 1943, during 'Blitz Week', one of the ninety-two Fortresses attacking Hannover was *Ruthie II*, piloted by Lieutenant Robert L. Campbell and his co-pilot, Flight Officer John C. Morgan, a six-foot, red-haired Texan. The navigator, Keith J. Koske, wrote later:

We were on our way into the enemy coast, when we were attacked by a group of Fw 190s. On their first pass I felt sure they had got us for there was a terrific explosion overhead

The old World War II control tower at Alconbury in October 1997.
(Mike Fuenfer)

and the ship rocked badly. A second later the top-turret gunner Staff Sergeant Tyre C. Weaver fell through the hatch and slumped to the floor at the rear of my nose compartment. When I got to him I saw his left arm had been blown off at the shoulder and he was a mass of blood. I first tried to inject some morphine but the needle was bent and I could not get it in.

As things turned out it was best I didn't give him any morphine. My first thought was to try and stop his loss of blood. I tried to apply a tourniquet but it was impossible as the arm was off too close to the shoulder. I knew he had to have the right kind of medical treatment as soon as possible and we had almost four hours flying time ahead of us, so there was no alternative. I opened the escape hatch, adjusted his chute for him and placed the ripcord ring firmly in his right hand. He must have become excited and pulled the cord, opening the pilot's chute in the updraft. I managed to gather it together and tuck it under his right arm, got him into a crouched position with legs through the hatch, made certain again that his good arm was holding the chute folds together, and toppled him out into space. I learned somewhat later from our ball turret gunner, James L. Ford, that the chute opened okay. We were at 24,500 feet and 25 miles due west of Hannover and our only hope was that he was found and given medical attention immediately.

The bombardier, Asa J. Irwin, had been busy with the nose guns and when I got back up in the nose he was getting ready to toggle his bombs. The target area was one mass of smoke and we added our contribution. After we dropped our bombs we were kept busy with the nose guns. However, all our attacks were from the tail and we could do very little good. I had tried to use my interphone several times, but could get no answer. The last I remember hearing over it was shortly after the first attack when someone was complaining about not getting oxygen. Except for what I thought to be some violent evasive action, we seemed to be flying okay.

It was two hours later when we were 15 minutes out from

the enemy coast that I decided to go up and check with the pilot and have a look around. I found Lieutenant Campbell slumped down in his seat, a mass of blood, and the back of his head blown off. This had happened 'two hours' before, on the first attack. A shell had entered from the right side, crossed in front of John Morgan, and had hit Campbell in the head. Morgan was flying the plane with one hand, holding the half-dead pilot off with the other hand and he had been doing it for over two hours! (It was no mean feat; Campbell was a six-footer who weighed 185 lb.) Morgan told me we had to get Campbell out of his seat as the plane couldn't be landed from the co-pilot's seat since the glass on that side was shattered so badly you could barely see out. We struggled for 30 minutes getting the fatally injured pilot out of his seat and down into the rear of the navigator's compartment, where the bombardier held him from slipping out of the open bomb doors. Morgan was operating the controls with one hand and helping me handle the pilot with the other.

The radio operator, waist and tail gunners were unable to lend assistance because they were unconscious through lack of oxygen, the lines having been shattered several hours earlier. Morgan's action was nothing short of miraculous. Not only had he flown the aircraft to the target and out again with no radio, no intercom and no hydraulic fluid, he had maintained formation the whole time; an incredible feat for a pilot flying one-handed.

Morgan brought *Ruthie II* in to land at RAF Foulsham, a few miles inland of the Norfolk coast and put down safely. Campbell died one and half hours after they reached England. The other crewmembers survived, including Weaver who had been put in a PoW camp after hospitalisation. On 18 December 1943, listeners to the BBC's evening news heard that Flight Officer (later 2/Lieutenant) John C. Morgan (now with the 482nd Bomb Group) had received the Medal of Honor from General Eaker in a special ceremony at 8th Air Force HQ and heard him relive the moments of 26 July.

From 10 to 22 September 1943 the 92nd Bomb Group began

moving to Podington to make room for the 482nd Bomb Group (H), which was formed at Alconbury to develop 'pathfinder' techniques for bombing through cloud with radar. This Group was unique in that it was the only 8th Air Force group to be officially activated in Britain. Two of its squadrons were equipped with the B-17F and G aircraft and one with B-24H, J and L aircraft fitted with *H2X*, *H2S*, *Oboe* and *APS-15A* and *Eagle* devices. The 482nd flew its first combat mission on 27 September 1943 and went on to provide pathfinder lead aircraft for other bomb groups throughout the winter of 1943–4. The 482nd flew its last combat mission on 22 March 1944 and became an operational training and development unit for various radar devices.

From 1946–51 Alconbury was an RAF bomb disposal site and aircraft maintenance depot. The US 3rd Air Force took over the airfield in August 1951 for development. From September 1955 until August 1959 it was a B-45 base. C-47s, C-54s and SA-16s of a Troop Carrier unit were also based there from May 1957. The 10th Tactical Reconnaissance Wing operated various aircraft between 1959 and 1987, including A-10s of the redesignated 10 TFW in the summer of 1988.

Bassingbourn (Station 121), Cambridgeshire

Around the top of the room, all the way around were all the Varga girls from a Varga calendar, put out by a plumbing concern, I think. There were also a good many pictures of girls in various stages of undress and discomfort, drawn by an artist with a mischievous mind, but a modest one . . . On top of the locker there was a picture of a girl Sam wanted to lure into marriage, maybe. Anyway, she was a dream, and some people didn't believe she was even Sam's girl. But I did . . .

The sacks were RAF sacks, because the whole rig used to belong to the RAF once, the whole station did. It was nice of them to let us live there, because it was probably the best room in England, even if that sergeant did take his radio back . . . On the wall above my sack was the map with all the places I've been in Europe. Some of the towns are left out on the map, so I have to draw in the bomb in the approximate place where our formation left a big hole . . . .

We were lucky to live in such a place.

England was always out the window, and I often thought I'd like to live in that room again for a while after the war, and wander around and see what the country's like in peacetime.

This extract from 'Co-Pilots' House' in *Serenade to the Big Bird*, the classic World War II tale penned by Bert Stiles, a co-pilot in 1/Lieutenant Samuel Newton's crew in the 401st Bomb Squadron in the 91st Bomb Group, aptly describes Bassing-bourn, where he flew a thirty-five-mission tour, from 19 April to 20 July 1944. (Stiles completed his bomber tour but instead of returning to America on the leave now due to him, he asked to be transferred to fighters, and he moved to the 339th Fighter Group and to P-51s. At the age of 23, he was shot down and killed on 26 November 1944, while escorting bombers to Hannover).

B-17G 42-97234 *Bomber Dear* of the 322nd Bomb Squadron, 91st Bomb Group, at Bassingbourn. This aircraft and Lieutenant Donald R. Sparkman's crew failed to return on 2 November 1944. Six men were KIA and three were taken into captivity. *(USAF)*

Control tower at Bassingbourn in October 1997. The wartime control tower has been turned into a memorial museum for both RAF and American units that were based at Bassingbourn. A section of the American display in the tower features the famed *Memphis Belle*. *(Mike Fuenfer)*

Bassingbourn airfield, built originally as a grass aerodrome for the RAF in a very shallow, wide valley north of Royston by John Laing & Son Ltd, opened in 1938. It had four brick and steel C-type hangars set in a crescent along the south-eastern corner of the airfield and the technical, communal and barrack buildings were adjacent to the hangars in a large block site extending south beside the A14. Some of the technical buildings were built of reinforced concrete and the barrack block buildings had flat concrete roofs. In 1942, work on bringing the aerodrome to Class A standard was started. Contractors W. & C. French Ltd extended the runways and increased the number of hardstandings to fifty-four, some of them on a taxiway extension, which crossed the A14. Additional barracks were built in dispersed sites to accommodate a total of 443 officers and 2529 men. Bassingbourn was used initially by 35, 98, 104, 108 and 215 Squadrons of the RAF during the early part of the war, until October 1942 when the ground echelon of the 17th Bomb Group

B-17G 42-32076 *Shoo Shoo Baby* of the 401st Bomb Squadron, 91st Bomb Group, was named by its crew after a popular song of the day. On 29 May 1944 it took Lieutenant Paul McDuffee's crew to Frankfurt on the first of twenty-four combat missions in which it was damaged by flak on seven occasions. Its last mission was to Poznan, Poland, on 29 May 1944, when engine problems forced Lieutenant Robert Guenther's crew to make a landing in neutral Sweden. The Swedish government was officially given seven B-17s as a gift, and in exchange American crews were repatriated. *Shoo Shoo Baby*'s nose was lengthened by 3 feet and accommodation provided for fourteen passengers and 4400 lb of cargo in the bomb bay. In 1955, after Swedish and Danish airline service and Danish military use, the aircraft was bought by a New York company and sold to the Institute Geographique National in Paris. In July 1978 *Shoo Shoo Baby* was flown by C-5 Galaxy to Dover Air Force Base, Delaware. After a ten-year restoration to flying condition, it was flown to the USAF Museum at Wright Patterson Air Force Base, Dayton, Ohio, on 13 October 1988, where *Shoo Shoo Baby* is now on permanent display. *(via Frank Thomas)*

The *Memphis Belle* pub at Bassingbourn. *(Author)*

B-17G 42-97061 *General Ike* in the 91st Bomb Group at Bassingbourn. *(USAF)*

At Bassingbourn B-17F 41-24485, better known as the *Memphis Belle* and piloted by Captain Robert K. Morgan, became legendary. The crew flew the twenty-fifth and final mission of their tour on 17 May 1943, to Lorient, and it was duly recorded (using a 'stand-in' B-17F) in 16-mm colour film and used with great effect in the documentary. Everyone, it seemed, wanted to meet the famous ten men of the *Memphis Belle*. On 26 May they were introduced to HM King George VI and HM Queen Elizabeth at Bassingbourn and on 13 June Generals Devers and Eaker paid them a visit and then bade them a Stateside farewell to take part in a bond tour of the USA. *(USAF)*

(Medium) equipped with B-26 Marauders spent a short sojourn after arriving from the USA.

On 14 October the 91st Bomb Group, with thirty-two B-17Fs, arrived from Kimbolton where the runways, having been built for RAF medium bombers, were totally unsuitable for Fortresses. The 91st Bomb Group flew only three practice missions from Kimbolton before Colonel Stanley Wray, the CO, decided that Bassingbourn was an ideal base for his bombers and 'Wray's Ragged Irregulars' as they became known, settled in. The air base, unlike most of the American airfields in Britain, which were remote and in the main inhospitable, proved a lure

Hollywood movie star Major Clark Gable poses with Lieutenant George Birdsong's crew of B-17F 42-5077 *Delta Rebel No. 2* of the 323rd Bomb Squadron, 91st Bomb Group, while shooting sequences for the documentary 'Combat America'. *Delta Rebel No. 2* and 2/Lieutenant Robert W. Thompson's crew FTR on 12 August 1943. Four crew were killed and six men were made PoW. *(USAF)*

for visiting pressmen, Hollywood film makers and general staff.

Major William Wyler, the famous Hollywood director who had produced *Mrs Miniver* in 1941, was sent to England late in 1942 to make a documentary about 8th Air Force operations, principally for American cinema audiences. Filming began early in 1943 after bad weather had delayed its start. Several B-17 crews were close to being the first to complete a twenty-five-mission combat tour and return home. One Fortress that caught Wyler's lens more than most, probably because of its emotive and eye-catching name, was the *Memphis Belle*, piloted by Captain Robert K. Morgan. During crew training he had met

B-17s of the 91st Bomb Group taxi out at Bassingbourn, in May 1944.
The aircraft at the right is *Little Patches*, which survived the war.
(USAF)

B-17 Flying Fortresses passing Bassingbourn airfield at sunrise.
(USAF)

B-17s in the hangar at Bassingbourn as night falls. *(USAF)*

A visiting Lockheed P-38 Lightning taxis around the perimeter track at Bassingbourn. The 1st and 14th Fighter Groups were originally assigned to 8th Fighter Command, but were reassigned to the 12th Air Force in September, while the 20th Fighter Group, which flew its first combat mission from King's Cliffe, Northamptonshire, on 28 December 1943, converted to P-51 Mustangs in July 1944. The 55th Fighter Group flew its first combat mission from Nuthampstead on 15 October 1943, also converting to the Mustang in July 1944. The 78th Fighter Group flew P-38Gs from December 1942 until February 1943, when it converted to P-47C Thunderbolts. *(USAF)*

On 11 April 1944 General Dwight D. Eisenhower christened B-17G
42-97061 *General Ike* with a bottle of Mississippi River water at
Bassingbourn. Major James McPartlin, 401st Bomb Squadron, was
responsible for the naming of *General Ike*, which flew its first
operational mission on 13 April 1944, two days after it was christened.
On 29 May 1944 *General Ike* led the 91st Bomb Group to Poznan,
Poland, on the longest daylight raid of the war up to that time. *General
Ike* completed seventy-five combat missions, returned to the USA in
June 1945 and was broken up for scrap. *(USAF)*

Miss Margaret Polk of Memphis, Tennessee, and the romance
had flourished for a time. Morgan and Polk later married other
partners, but the legendary artwork remained indelibly painted
on the nose of the B-17 through thick and thin. Five combat
photographers were lost aboard B-17s during filming.
Eventually, the finale to the film loomed large as the crew of the
Memphis Belle neared its twenty-fifth and final mission of their
tour. *Memphis Belle* was not the first to complete an 8th Air
Force tour, but its twenty-fifth mission on 17 May 1943, to
Lorient, was duly recorded (using a 'stand-in' B-17F) in 16-mm

B-17F 42-5225 *Stormy Weather of the* 323rd Bomb Squadron, 91st Bomb Group, survived an encounter with German fighters on 4 March 1943, but returned to Bassingbourn with one engine on fire and overshot the runway. The aircraft was repaired and flew again, being renamed *V-Packette* in July 1943, only to be lost on the first Schweinfurt raid on 17 August 1943, when it was flown by 2/Lieutenant Don Van Der Heyde. *(USAF)*

colour film and used with great effect in the documentary. Everyone, it seemed, wanted to meet the famous ten men of the *Memphis Belle.* On 26 May they were introduced to HRH King George VI and Queen Elizabeth at Bassingbourn and on 9 June General Ira Eaker paid them a visit and then bade them a Stateside farewell to take part in a National War Bond tour of US cities lasting ninety days. What finally emerged in April 1945 was a colourful and exciting thirty-eight-minute masterpiece, which Britons saw for the first time in the winter of 1944–5.

On 11 April 1944 during a ceremony held at Bassingbourn General Dwight D. Eisenhower, Supreme Commander, SHAEF christened a B-17G named *GENERAL IKE* in his honour with a bottle of Mississippi River water. On *GENERAL IKE*'s sixty-fifth mission, a windmilling No. 3 propeller sheared off and sliced into the nose-art, but miraculously no one was even scratched.

The 91st Bomb Group flew all of its 340 combat missions from Bassingbourn from 7 November 1942 to 25 April 1945. The

American servicemen and Red Cross personnel gather in front of John Bunyan's statue in Bedford. The county town was a bustling 'Liberty Town' for the thousands of troops and airmen stationed nearby who frequented the pubs and dance halls and the American Red Cross Officers' and Enlisted Men's Clubs. *(Bedford Archives)*

B-17F 41-24524 *The Eagle's Wrath* of the 323rd Bomb Squadron, 91st Bomb Group, at Bassingbourn, which failed to return with Lieutenant Anthony G. Arcaro's crew on the 17 August 1943 mission to Schweinfurt. *(USAF)*

Group dropped just over 22,142 tons of bombs, losing 197 Fortresses, the highest loss of all 8th Air Force bomb groups. The Group led the first Schweinfurt mission on 17 August 1943, losing ten of its thirty-one B-17s, and was the first 8th Air Force bomb group to complete 100 missions. It also had the highest total claims of enemy aircraft destroyed by the 1st Bombardment Division and two Distinguished Unit Citations.

In September 1951 Bassingbourn returned to RAF occupancy, though some American units did TDY at the airfield during times of crisis. During the Korean War the 301st Bomb Group (H) arrived with B-29s and in 1951 RB-50Bs were based there with B-50Ds of the 97th Bomb Group. When 231 OCU (Operational Conversion Unit), a Canberra training unit, left, the airfield closed on 19 May 1969. On 29 August Bassingbourn became a major British Army Infantry Training Depot with the arrival of the HQ and Depot The Queen's Division. In 1993 the Depot became one of five Army Training Regiments responsible for Phase 1 or Basic Training for the Royal Corps of Signals, the Queen's Division of Infantry and the Royal Logistics Corps.

3

Bovingdon (Station 112), Hertfordshire

Built by John Laing & Son Ltd in 1941–42 as a bomber airfield, the main NE-SW runway was 1634 yards long and two subsidiary runways were each 1433 yards long. Extending into the woods at the north of the airfield were over thirty dispersal areas. However, the airfield was never developed to Class A standard. On 15 June 1942 the station was taken over by 7 Group, RAF Bomber Command. Though the 92nd Bomb Group arrived in August 1942, Bovingdon was not officially transferred to the 8th Air Force until 28 April 1943. The 92nd Bomb Group was the first heavy bombardment group successfully to make a non-stop flight to England, but on arrival the men were disappointed in the physical appearance of the unfinished base.

The barracks required strenuous cleaning, the sanitary facilities were poor and those for bathing almost non-existent – the sites on which the various squadrons lived did not have bathhouses and the communal site with its one bathhouse was sadly overtaxed. Food, upon the Group's arrival and for about four weeks, was strictly

Control tower at Bovingdon in October 1997. *(Mike Fuenfer)*

British and the menus monotonously featured mutton, potatoes and Brussels Sprouts.

The 92nd was not put on operational status, but instead was assigned the role of a B-17 Combat Crew Replacement Unit (CCRC). Just four combat missions and three diversions were flown from the airfield before three of the 92nd Bomb Group's squadrons transferred to Alconbury on 4 January 1943. Only the 326th Squadron and some key personnel were left at Bovingdon to form the 11th CCRC for providing theatre indoctrination training for combat crews newly arrived in Britain. In September 1944 the CCRC disbanded and the airfield became the base for the European Air Transport Service. After the war, Bovingdon airfield was used by military communication aircraft serving the US 3rd Air Division HQ at South Ruislip until 1962 and RAF Fighter Command HQ at Bentley Priory. In 1961 Bovingdon, appropriately, was used to stage action sequences involving B-17s for the film *The War Lover*, which starred Steve McQueen and Robert Wagner. In 1964 this was followed by Mosquitoes used for flying sequences in *633 Squadron* and again in 1964 by the sequel *Mosquito Squadron*. In 1968 it was announced by the Ministry of Defence that Bovingdon would close. In 1972 the renovated hangars were torn down and all MoD property, except some married quarters, were disposed of by 1976. Some buildings were transferred to the Home Office for use as a Youth Custody Centre.

An American Red Cross Clubmobile (a converted British bus) serves refreshments to ground crews of the 92nd Bomb Group working on B-17F 41-9020 *Phyllis* at Bovingdon, from where it made several courier flights to North Africa late in 1942. Clubmobiles were first introduced in 1942 and were manned by Red Cross girls who dispensed cups of hot coffee, cigarettes, chewing gum, doughnuts and newspapers free of charge. By the end of 1943, there were fifty in operation, each servicing detachments six miles or more from a club. The 92nd Bomb Group acted as a Combat Crew Replacement Centre for 8th Bomber Command and did not fly its first combat mission until 6 September 1943. *Phyllis* had previously served in the 97th Bomb Group and on 1 May 1943 was assigned to the 303rd Bomb Group at Molesworth. *(USAF)*

4

Cheddington (Station 113), Hertfordshire

Cheddington airfield was built as a satellite for Bovingdon by George Wimpey & Co. Ltd. Though never brought up to Class A standard (the main runway was only 1780 yards long), it was made available to the 8th Air Force and in September 1942 the 44th Bomb Group's Liberators arrived from the USA. Their stay was brief, however, and in October 'The Flying Eightballs' moved to their permanent base at Shipdham in Norfolk. Cheddington became the 12th Combat Crew Replacement Centre, specialising in the operational training of B-24 aircrews and additionally, from March 1945, for fighter training. On 24 June 1944 the Night Leaflet Squadron (858th, later the 406th Bomb Squadron) arrived from Chelveston and remained until March 1945, when it moved to Harrington. During operations from England this unit's B-17s and B-24s dropped 1800 million leaflets and news sheets on 7000 targets in 330 night missions. The Radio Countermeasures Squadrons (36th Bomb Squadron) was also based at Cheddington from 14 August 1944 to 28 February 1945. Cheddington was also the Headquarters station of 8th Air Force Composite Command when this organisation was transferred to the UK from Northern Ireland. On 21 June 1945 Cheddington was returned to RAF

Bomber Command and became part of 26 Group on 6 July. After further use by Technical and Medical Training on 13 August 1946, the station was renamed RAF Marsworth. The Medical Unit left on 16 February 1948 when the station was closed. The airfield became inactive and slowly fell into disrepair, although Central Intelligence Agency personnel were once stationed here. The CIA left suddenly in 1963 when media attention was focused on the area five miles away at Linslade Farm and the London to Edinburgh railway line following the 'Great Train Robbery'.

5

Chelveston (Station 105), Northamptonshire

Construction of Chelveston airfield began in 1940 by Taylor-Woodrow Ltd and it was intended for occupation by 8 Group RAF. However, the airfield was used by the Central Gunnery School and then for trials of troop-carrying gliders, until in 1942 the base was reallocated to the USAAF. Two T2 hangars and a J-type hangar were erected, but the runways were too short for American bombers and they had to be extended and additional taxiways and hardstands added. The first American unit to occupy the base was the 60th Troop Carrier Group whose fifty-three C-47 transport aircraft arrived in July 1942, though their stay was short as the Group had moved to Aldermaston by the end of that month. In August the air and ground echelons of the 301st Bomb Group, the second of the 8th Air Force's heavy bomb groups in England, arrived with B-17Fs. Three of the Group's squadrons operated from Chelveston while for a time the ground echelon of the 352nd Bomb Squadron was based at Podington. The 301st Bomb Group flew its first combat mission on 5 September, to the Rouen marshalling yards in northern France, but only another seven missions were flown from Chelveston.

One of the most famous entertainers to visit England in wartime was undoubtedly Bob Hope, seen here with singer Frances Langford and Tony Romano with the Sam Johnstone's crew in the 364th Bomb Squadron, 305th Bomb Group, at Chelveston in front of B-17F *Lallah VIII* on 5 July 1943. This aircraft and Ellsworth F. Kenyon's were shot down on the mission to Schweinfurt on 14 October 1943. *(USAF via Bill Donald)*

This mural by British artist Bruce Bairnsfather, who created the famous Great War character Old Bill, once adorned the wall of the Officers' Club at Chelveston. Bairnsfather contributed cartoons to the US Army newspaper *Stars & Stripes* in World War II. One of the 365th Bomb Squadron, 305th Bomb Group's B-17Fs was named *Old Bill* in honour of the cartoon character. *(via Bill Donald)*

B-17F 41-24614 *We The People*, of the 422nd Bomb Squadron, 305th Bomb Group, at Chelveston on 7 March 1943, with the pilot, Captain Cliff Pyle, far right. In more than thirty missions it never carried exactly the same crew twice and no crewman was ever wounded. On 8 September 1943 it led the first 8th Air Force night-bombing mission of the war, returning to the ZOI on 31 May 1945. *(Cliff Pyle)*

The Group, which with the 97th Bomb Group was one of two in England selected to support the invasion of North Africa, flew its last mission on 8 November before departing for the Mediterranean Theatre. In early December 1942 Chelveston airfield was occupied by the 305th Bomb Group, which flew in from Grafton Underwood, or Grafton 'Undermud' as crew preferred to call it, where reconstruction work was planned. The 305th Bomb Group , known as the 'Can Do' Group, was commanded at the time by Colonel Curtis E. LeMay, who was to become a legendary figure in the US Air Forces in World War II, first in Europe and then the Far East. LeMay helped pioneer many of the techniques of day bomber-formation procedures and precision bombing, which were later adopted as standard operating procedures in the US air forces. In the

B-17F-55-BO 42-29529 *Nora II* of the 364th Bomb Squadron at
Chelveston with 1/Lieutenant Lester Personeus's crew, which had
flown fifteen missions together and went on to finish with twenty-five
missions apiece. *Nora II* transferred to the 384th Bomb Group and
2/Lieutenant G. J. Poole crash-landed the aircraft at Grafton
Underwood on 13 December 1943. *(USAF via Bill Donald)*

late summer of 1943, the 422nd Bomb Squadron experimented
with night bombing and dropping leaflets at night and in 1944,
the squadron extended its activities to pathfinder techniques
with *H2X* airborne radar. The first of two Distinguished Unit
Citations was awarded to the 305th Bomb Group for its part in
a raid on Paris on 4 April 1943, the second on 11 January 1944.

The 305th Bomb Group led the raid on Schweinfurt on 14
October 1943, when the Group lost thirteen aircraft. In early 1944
the Medal of Honor was awarded to two pilots in the 364th
Bomb Squadron who after their B-17s had been attacked head-
on by fighters and they were wounded, managed to get their
battered B-17s home again and land them. 1/Lieutenant William
R. Lawley Jr was awarded the Medal of Honor for bringing his

B-17G 44-6009 *Flak Eater* of the 364th Bomb Squadron, 305th Bomb Group, at Chelveston with shark teeth adorning the chin turret. This Fortress failed to return, landing on the Continent on 4 December 1944. Subsequently repaired and flown back, *Flak Eater* returned to the ZOI and was scrapped in 1945. *(USAF)*

B-17F 42-30375, *Yo-Yo 'It Always Comes Back'*, of the 366th Bomb Squadron, 305th Bomb Group at Chelvston. Lt. Jack Kney and his crew on completion of their 25th mission. Howard Jack Kney and his crew volunteered to fly more missions and were allocated to other groups. Kney was killed in 1944. (USAF via Bill Donald)

'Target for Tonight' was a favourite expression used by RAF Bomber Command crews. Its American derivation, where the 'target for tonite' was a 'hot date', is a double meaning used to adorn the Fortress flown by Lieutenant Verle's crew in the 305th Bomb Group at Chelveston in March 1944. *(USAF via Bill Donald)*

badly shot up B-17 home on 20 February and 1/Lieutenant Edward S. Michael brought *Bertie Lee* home on 11 April after it had been devastated by cannon fire and had plummeted into a 3000-foot dive.

A total of 337 missions was flown by the 305th Bomb Group between 1 November 1942 and 25 April 1945 for the loss of 154 aircraft missing in action. Selected for duty with the Air Force of Occupation, the 305th Bomb Group moved first to St Trond, Belgium, and later to Germany, where it was finally disbanded in 1946. Chelveston, meanwhile, had reverted to RAF control in October 1945 when it became a satellite for 25 Maintenance Unit. It was returned to US Air Force use on 1 December 1952 and a new, extra-long, runway was laid and new facilities constructed. Although the airfield did have some flying units for short periods, the base served as a readiness base to receive USAF units from the US in an emergency. An American presence was maintained by the 2130th Communications Group, which operated a radio station in a fenced-off enclosure. Near the airfield a housing estate was provided for US personnel serving at the bases of Alconbury and Molesworth.

6

Deenethorpe (Station 128), Northamptonshire

This base on part of the Brudenell Estate, which dates back several hundred years and is a famous family name with Crimean War and the Charge of the Light Brigade connections, was built in 1942–3 alongside the A427 between Corby and Oundle. Main contractors John Laing & Son Ltd built the airfield to conform to the RAF Class A heavy bomber standard, but in October 1943 it was allocated to the USAAF. A 2000-yard main runway and two 1400-yard runways, fifty dispersed hardstandings adjoining the perimeter track and two T2-type hangars were built. Living accommodation and domestic quarters for 2894 men were provided in temporary huts dispersed on either side of the A427 to the south of the airfield stretching into Upper Benefield. In October 1943 Deenethorpe was occupied by the 401st Bomb Group, which was equipped with B-17G Fortresses and commanded by Colonel Harold W. Bowman. The Group flew the first of its 255 combat missions on 26 November when nineteen Fortresses led by Colonel Bowman raided Bremen, though four aircraft did not become airborne. One ran off the perimeter track, trapping the following aircraft, and two more collided due to brake failure. During their eighteen-month stay the 401st Bomb Group lost ninety-four B-17s, the second lowest

The control tower at Deenethorpe in 1970 with the words, 'Flying Control' at the top. *(Author)*

loss rate of all 8th Air Force Fortress groups. In July 1944 the 401st Bomb Group led the entire 8th Air Force in bombing accuracy and tied with the 303rd Bomb Group during the period May to July when both groups dropped 61 per cent of their bombs within 1000 feet of the MPI.

On Sunday 5 December 1943 at 0830 hours *Zenodia El Elephanta*, piloted by Lieutenant Walter B. Keith, iced up and slewed on take-off, careering over farmland and coming to rest on top of a barn on the edge of Deenethorpe village. The tail of the B-17 had broken off with Sergeant Bob Kerr inside but he escaped unhurt. Eight of the crew just had time to evacuate the wreckage and warn the villagers before the bomb load exploded. (The navigator and bombardier, trapped in the front of the aircraft, were rescued by ground personnel from the base and eventually recovered from their injuries.) Twenty minutes after crashing, the bomb load detonated, damaging many houses in the village but, incredibly, no lives were lost. The blast was felt in Kettering, twelve miles away.

The 401st Bomb Group gained two Distinguished Unit Citations, the first for a raid on Oschersleben on 11 January 1944, when the Group lost four B-17s, and the other for a raid on Leipzig on 20 February 1944. The most famous B-17 of the 401st Bomb Group was 42-31983 *Mary Alice* of the 615th Bomb Squadron. Its first raid was on Berlin and its ninety-eighth and last mission was on 19 April 1945. Reputed to have been the most battle-damaged Fortress in the 8th Air Force, *Mary Alice* was flown home to the United States at the end of the war and was scrapped in Arizona. (A replica *Mary Alice* can be seen in the American Museum at the Imperial War Museum Duxford, resplendent in the markings of the 401st Bomb Group.) Two other B-17s that achieved over 100 missions were 42-97395 *Chute the Works* of the 614th Squadron, which achieved 111 missions and crashed near Sawtry on 25 March 1945, and 42-31730 of the

The most famous B-17 at Deenethorpe was *Mary Alice* of the 615th Bomb Squadron, 401st Bomb Group. Reputed to have been the most battle-damaged Fortress in the 8th Air Force, *Mary Alice* was flown home to the United States at the end of the war and was scrapped in Arizona. A replica *Mary Alice* can be seen in the American Museum at the IWM Duxford, resplendent in the markings of the 401st Bomb Group. *(Author)*

B-17Gs of the 401st Bomb Group at a wintry Deenethorpe on 12
January 1945. The nearest aircraft is B-17G 43-38077 *DUKE'S
MIXTURE* in the 615th Bomb Squadron. This aircraft was later
reassigned to the 614th Bomb Squadron and renamed *Tag A Long*. It
finished its days at Kingman, Arizona, in November 1945. *(USAF)*

615th Squadron, with 112 missions, which returned to the ZOI in
June 1945.

The 401st Bomb Group returned to the US in late May to early
June 1945 and the RAF occupied Deenethorpe on 20 June as 11
Recruiting Centre. This officially closed in mid-1946. The airfield
was gradually returned to agriculture, though for several years
the runway was used as an emergency landing strip for RAF
aircraft. Part of the 6000-foot runway is now used as a private
airstrip for executive aircraft for the British Steelworks at Corby
who resurfaced it in the late 1960s.

7

Glatton (Conington) (Station 130), Huntingdonshire

This airfield, which took the name Glatton because Conington might have been confused with an existing airfield at Coningsby in Lincolnshire, was built during 1942–3 by the 809th Engineer Battalion (Aviation) of the US Army, with assistance from local contractors. Bill Ong, a US Army engineer involved in building airfields in England, recalls some of the statistics of all the work done at Glatton. 'Concrete laid, 122,000 cubic yards. Sewer lines, 22,000 feet. Water lines, 29,500 feet. French drains, 24,400 feet. Buildings, 500 of all kinds. Water supply, 120,000 gallons per day. Storm sewers, 67,000 feet. Electric wiring, 450,000 feet. Telephone system, 2,000 calls per day. Sewage plant, 8,000 people per day.' Glatton airfield was only 20 feet above sea level and the continuing rain made drainage almost impossible. The airfield was located between the LNER East Coast main railway line from London to the north of England and the A1 Great North Road, an old Roman road called Ermine Street. The layout of the base with three runways, encircling perimeter track, fifty

Colonel James R. Luper, CO 457th Bomb Group, brought the badly damaged *Rene III* home from Ludwigshaven on 27 May 1944 and crash-landed at Glatton on only one wheel. Colonel Luper was shot down on the Politz raid on 7 October 1944 and he became a prisoner-of-war. *(USAF)*

loop-type hardstands and temporary buildings, was unique in that Rose Court Farm (which still exists) continued to operate in the centre of the airfield. Two T2 hangars were erected with other technical and administrative buildings built in concrete, brick, steel and asbestos. Living accommodation for 421 officers and 2473 men was dispersed in the countryside around the village of Conington to the south-west of the airfield.

On 21 January 1944 the air echelon of the 457th Bomb Group (H), the last B-17 Fortress Group assigned to the 1st Division, flew in from the US. The ground echelon arrived in the early hours of 2 February, disembarking from trains at Holme Station about a mile from the airfield. The Group flew the first of 237 missions on 21 February. The 'Fireball Outfit', as it was called, lost its first commanding officer, Colonel James R. Luper, on 7 October 1944, when he was shot down on the Politz raid and became a prisoner–of-war. The Group flew 7086 sorties, with nearly 17,000 tons of bombs and 142 tons of leaflets being dropped, and flew its last mission on 20 April 1945. Some eighty-three Fortresses were lost – missing in action. One of the worst days was the mission to the synthetic oil refinery at Merseburg on 2 November 1944 when the 'Fireball Outfit' lost nine B-17s, including six from the 751st Bomb Squadron flying as the low squadron. Merseburg soon became the main topic of conversation among the old-timers at Glatton. When Ken Blakeborough, a replacement pilot, arrived at Glatton on Christmas Eve 1944, he was quick to notice it. Blakeborough threw his baggage on an empty bunk and was told by one of the old-timers in the 'Fireball Outfit' that the bed he had chosen had belonged to Gordon Gallagher, who had gone down at Merseburg on 2 November flying *Prop Wash*. Blakeborough observed that combat losses were rather hushed up; he did not know whether by intent or not. 'Unless you knew someone who'd gone down you didn't ever hear about losses.' By VE Day Blakeborough had flown thirty-two missions, was awarded an Air Medal and four clusters and was sent home. His stay in England was a brief seven months, but he recalled that they were indelibly part of his life. On 11 May 1945 there was a VE Day parade and service in Peterborough cathedral, which was attended by representatives from all units at Station 130.

Glatton was handed over to the RAF on 12 July 1945 and soon became No. 70 Transit Camp for homecoming Allied PoWs. Three weeks later a practice landing by twenty-six Lancasters took place as a rehearsal for Operation *Dodge*, which went ahead on 1 August. During the month nearly 13,000 ex-PoWs were ferried to Glatton in fleets of Lancasters and Liberators. On one day, 20 August, no fewer than seventy-nine Lancasters and fourteen Liberators arrived at the base and they had to be parked 'nose to tail' because of space restrictions. Operation *Dodge* finished on 15 January 1946, by which time No. 70 Transit Camp had processed 36,799 passengers. The camp closed in March 1946.

Situated close to the north of the airfield is Holmewood Hall, which in World War II was known as 'Area H', a US Office of Strategic Services (OSS) training, supply and packing centre. The packing station in the grounds at Holme covered a huge area from which canisters containing supplies, weapons and ammunition were transported to Special Operations Executive (SOE) at RAF Tempsford and to the 801st Carpetbagger unit at Harrington. The packed canisters left Holme in covered trucks either hired from or painted as London Brick Company vehicles.

8

Grafton Underwood (Station 106) Northamptonshire

Construction of an airfield at Grafton Underwood, originally planned as one of a number of hard-surfaced bomber stations for 8 Group, RAF, began in 1941 by George Wimpey & Co. Ltd who laid runways and hard-standings. The main runway was approximately 1600 yards and two others were 1100 yards in length. In 1942, with the imminent arrival of the US 8th Air Force in Britain, the runways were lengthened to handle operation of heavy, four-engined bombers such as the B-17. The main runway length was increased to 2000 yards and the other two to 1400 yards, while at the same time the thirty-four hardstandings were increased to fifty and two T2 hangars were built. Eleven dispersed sites, comprising the communal and barrack accommodation for 3000 men, were built in countryside to the east, while other facilities were expanded to cope with the arrival of the first 8th Air Force units. On 12 May 1942 the 15th Bomb Squadron arrived to begin training on Boston (A-20) light bombers on loan from the RAF, but as the airfield was far

B-17G 42-37781 *Silver Dollar* of the 546th Bomb Squadron, 384th Bomb Group, which bellied in at Grafton Underwood on 26 December 1943. After repairs *Silver Dollar* flew with the 544th and 545th Bomb Squadrons and went MIA with Lieutenant Merlin H. Reed's crew over Berlin on 9 March 1944 when the Fortress was hit by a bomb dropped from above. Eight men were KIA and two were made PoW. *(Joseph Minton via Larry Goldstein)*

from ready, a move to Molesworth was made early in June. The 15th Bomb Squadron had the honour of flying the first American mission from England on 4 July when six crews participated in joint USAAF–RAF raids on airfields in Holland by a formation of Boston IIIs. In turn, Grafton Underwood became famous as the base from which the first American heavy bomber raid from the UK was flown following the arrival, in July, of the 97th Bomb Group commanded by Colonel Cornelius Cousland. The ground echelon arrived in Scotland aboard the *Queen Elizabeth* on 9 June and entrained for Northamptonshire. After a stopover at Carlisle, the men detrained at Oundle and the 340th and 341st Squadrons travelled by bus to Polebrook, while the 342nd and 414th Squadrons left the train a Kettering and were bussed to Grafton Underwood. The first of the Group's B-17Es arrived in early July, but before the month was out Cousland had been sacked for running a 'lackadaisical, loose-jointed, fun-loving, badly trained outfit', which was 'in no sense ready for combat'.

Colonel Frank A. Armstrong arrived from VIII Bomber Command HQ to take over command. The former West Pointer and officers under his command like Major Paul Tibbets, Group Flying Executive Officer, instilled discipline and formulated tactics and training. The momentous first US heavy bomber raid went ahead on 17 August when twelve B-17s led by Armstrong and Tibbets in *Butcher Shop* took off from Grafton Underwood and bombed marshalling yards at Rouen, France. (Six B-17Es of the 340th and 341st Squadrons flew a diversionary mission.) On 8 September the 342nd and 414th Bomb Squadrons joined the rest of the 97th Bomb Group at Polebrook and the Group transferred to the 12th Air Force in North Africa in November.

On 12 September 1942 the air echelon of the 305th Bomb Group commanded by Colonel Curtis E. LeMay arrived at Grafton Underwood with B-17s and they flew their first mission on 17 November. Grafton 'Undermud' as it was known, was unsuitable for continued B-17 missions and in December the Group moved to Chelveston, which was in a more advanced state of completion. The next 8th Air Force heavy bomb group to arrive was the 96th Bomb Group, commanded by Colonel Archie J. Old, Jr, which flew in from the US during the latter part of April 1943. This Group commenced combat missions on 14

B-17G 43-38757 *Peasley's Payoff* of the 547th Bomb Squadron, 384th Bomb Group, which despite this mishap on 8 May 1945, was repaired and returned to the ZOI. *(USAF)*

May but its stay was short, as it was assigned to the 4th Wing in north Essex. The 96th Bomb Group began moving to Andrews Field towards the end of May.

The 384th Bomb Group arrived from the US and was based at Station 106 for the rest of the war, flying 314 missions between 22 June 1943 and 25 April 1945 and losing 159 aircraft and 1579 men missing in action. The Group was awarded two Distinguished Unit Citations, one, which went to all 1 Bomb Division Groups, for the raid on 11 January 1944 and the second for leading the 41st Combat Bombardment Wing through fierce enemy opposition to bomb an airfield and factory at Oberpfaffenhofen.

At the end of the war, in RAF hands again, Grafton Underwood became 236 Maintenance Unit, employing up to two hundred civilian drivers and mechanics, commanded by Squadron Leader Bradshaw. The unit was responsible for repairing and storing thousands of Air Ministry vehicles, which were sold at monthly, public auctions. The airfield was finally declared surplus to requirements and closed on 1 February 1959. The airfield forms part of the estate of the Duke of Buccleugh and most of the buildings remaining are used by Broughton Estates Ltd, a company owned by His Grace, although some are currently occupied by Agronomix.

9

Harrington (Station 179), Northamptonshire

The 826th and 852nd Engineer Battalions of the US Army built Harrington airfield in 1943 for heavy bomber use. In March 1944 it was chosen as the base for the 8th Air Force's 801st Bomb Group (Provisional), which was responsible for parachuting arms and equipment to resistance forces in France, the Low Countries and Norway. The 801st Bomb Group evolved from the 36th and 406th Bomb Squadrons, which were formed in November 1943 using personnel and B-24D Liberator aircraft from squadrons of the disbanded 479 Anti-Submarine Group and assigned to the 8th Air Force. The 36th and 406th Bomb Squadrons were activated at Alconbury on 4 December 1943. The first of sixty-three sorties delivering 153 tons of supplies were flown from Tempsford in January 1944 and were administered by the 482nd Bomb Group until 27 February 1944, when the black-painted Liberators moved to Watton, Norfolk. On 28 March the 801st Bomb Group, as it was now known, was assigned to AFCC. In April, agents or 'Joes' as they were called, began to be carried and were parachuted into enemy-occupied territory. A few C-47s were used to land agents in France. Two more squadrons were added and operations were flown almost entirely over occupied France and the Low Countries until

An all black Carpetbagger Liberator taking off from Harrington.
(USAF)

August, when the unit was renumbered the 492nd Bomb Group, taking the number of the disbanded Group at North Pickenham. As the Allied forces swept across the continent, full-scale operations were curtailed and eventually only one squadron was retained for limited Carpetbagger operations over Holland, Norway and Denmark. On 1 October the 801st Bomb Group was reassigned to VIII Fighter Command control. The 859 Bomb Squadron was dispatched to Italy and did not return, while in December 1944 the 857th and 858th Bomb Squadrons commenced night bombing sorties. The 857th Bomb Squadron aircraft and crews were absorbed by other units and the designation allotted to 1st Scouting Force at Bassingbourn. On 1 January 1945 the 492nd Bomb Group was assigned to the 1st Air Division. In March 1945 detachments from the 856th and 858th Bomb Squadrons were sent to Dijon, France, where eighty-two agents were parachuted into Germany with special radios whose transmitted messages could be picked up by 856th Bomb Squadron Mosquitoes on recording devices. Forty-six of these sorties were flown under the code names *Red Stocking* and

Skywave. A Distinguished Unit Citation was awarded to the 492nd Bomb Group for its work over Germany and German-occupied territory from 20 March to 25 April 1945.

From June to July 1945, the 492nd Bomb Group returned to the US and was deactivated on 17 October. Harrington gradually returned to farmland. In the early 1960s part of the airfield became one of the sites for the WS-315A Thor intermediate-range surface-to-surface ballistic missiles (IRBM) site and three launch pads and ancillary buildings were constructed. The 60-foot missile was powered by a 150,000-lb thrust Rocketdyne North American Aviation engine fuelled on liquid oxygen and RP-1 (a light-cut petrol) and had a range of 1500 nautical miles. It was adopted for use by twenty squadrons in the RAF in 1957 as Britain's nuclear deterrent until the entry into service of RAF V-bombers carrying nuclear missiles. Each squadron had three missiles, making a total of sixty deployed at bases throughout East Anglia and Yorkshire. The Thor was phased out of RAF service in August 1963 when the manned V-bombers came on stream and the missile sites were abandoned. Most of Harrington airfield, including the rocket site, is now owned and farmed by Merton College Oxford.

Kimbolton (Station 117), Huntingdonshire

Construction of this airfield was started in 1941 by W. & C. French Ltd. It was to accommodate RAF bombers, but the need for bases for American bombers saw the airfield gradually brought up to Class A standard. The first USAAF unit to occupy the airfield was the 91st Bomb Group, which arrived from the USA in September 1942. Its B-17s used Kimbolton for only a month because the base was often a sea of mud and the runways, having been built for RAF medium bombers, were considered totally unsuitable for four-engined bombers. The 91st

Lieutenant Colonel James Dubose with HRH Princess Elizabeth at Kimbolton on 6 July 1944. *(USAF)*

A badly wounded gunner in the 379th Bomb Group is given immediate medical treatment by the side of his Fortress. *(USAF)*

Bomb Group flew only three practice missions from Kimbolton before Colonel Stanley Wray, the CO, decided that Bassingbourn was an ideal base for his Fortresses. Another month passed as Kimbolton airfield became the temporary home for the ground echelon of the 17th Bomb Group (Medium) whose B-26 Marauders were destined for North Africa. During the 17th Bomb Group's sojourn, work on extending the main NW–SE runway began. The main runway was eventually extended from 1340 yards to 2000 yards and the hardstandings increased from thirty to fifty. Two T2s were erected (one on the western side and the other on the southern side of the airfield), while additional living sites were built close to Kimbolton village.

By the spring of 1943 Kimbolton was able to receive heavy bombers and the B-17F Fortresses of the 379th Bomb Group, commanded by Colonel Maurice 'Mo' A. Preston, flew in during late May and early June after a brief sojourn at Bovingdon for theatre indoctrination training. The 379th Bomb Group was to prove the most successful of all the 8th Air Force heavy bomber groups. Its success stemmed from the early leadership of Colonel Preston, who, according to Captain D. D. Robb in his book *Shades of Kimbolton*, '. . . turned the 379th from one of the greenest of the green outfits into the hottest bombing group in the 8th'. Colonel Preston, who commanded from 26 November 1942 to 10 October 1944, once said, 'If a unit wished to score well in bombing accuracy it was necessary to make a straight, unswerving bomb run with no evasive action to avoid flak; but this resulted in greater losses.'

Colonel (later General) Lewis E. Lyle, who commanded the

On 6 July 1944 King George VI, Queen Elizabeth and Princess Elizabeth visited the 379th Bomb Group base at Kimbolton, where they were introduced to the crew of B-17G 43-37777/Q *Four of a Kind* in the 525th Bomb Squadron. Here, Princess Elizabeth is pictured with Lieutenant-General James H. Doolittle. *Four of a Kind* (so named because of the last four digits of its serial number) was later transferred to the 527th Bomb Squadron and failed to return from a mission on 21 March 1945, having put down at an emergency landing strip on the Continent. *(Richards Collection)*

With one eye on the time, Lieutenant Colonel James Dubose escorts
HM King George VI, HM Queen Elizabeth and HRH Princess
Elizabeth and General Jimmy Doolittle around Kimbolton on 6 July
1944. *(USAF)*

A wedding at Kimbolton
on 4 November 1944.
(USAF)

379th Bomb Group from 11 October 1944 to 5 May 1945, paid tribute to the ground crews.

> They too were under a lot of pressure even though the danger wasn't there. A 16-hour day was kind of easy for them. There was just no end to the work. Sometimes they might get a plane ready at two in the morning, three days in a row, each time the mission getting cancelled because of weather. So the ground crews were constantly going through setting up a plane for a mission. Every day, there

B-17F 42-3524 *Vonnie Gal* of the 527th Bomb Squadron, 379th Bomb Group, pictured at Kimbolton shortly before noon on 5 June 1944. It was photographed by armourer/bombsight maintenance man Joe D'Angelo, using his Brownie box camera. 1/Lieutenant Jack Lamont, whose crew flew their second mission on this day in this aircraft, is walking almost beneath the nose. 1/Lieutenant Jack Lamont's crew flew twenty-seven or twenty-eight missions in this aircraft, which by July 1944 was the oldest operational Fortress in the Group. On its fiftieth mission, on 20 July, *Vonnie Gal* and 2/Lieutenant William F Moore's crew FTR from Leipzig. Hit by flak in the fuel lines just after bombs away, Moore put down at Payerne airfield, Switzerland. *Vonnie Gal* left Switzerland for Burtonwood on 25 September 1945.
(Joe D'Angelo via Richards)

B-17G 44-6507 *Lucky Patch* of the 527th Bomb Squadron, 379th Bomb Group, which crashed on 3 May 1945 when the landing gear collapsed. *(USAF)*

GIs of the 379th Bomb Group play ball at Kimbolton. In the background is B-17 42-38141 *Pansy Yokum* in the 524th Bomb Squadron, which ditched in the North Sea with Lieutenant Clarence E. Darnell's crew on 9 July 1944. *(USAF)*

British film actress Anna Neagle in front of B-17G 44-83288 *Lady Anna*
in the 527th Bomb Squadron, 379th Bomb Group, named in her
honour at Kimbolton in 1945. *(USAF)*

was a different fuel load, different bomb load. That's what
the war was for these guys. Their plane and the guy
working with him. If their plane came back shot up or
something, they just cried tears like babies. They loved that
airplane.

In all, the 379th Bomb Group flew 330 missions between 29
May 1943 and 25 April 1945 and dropped 26,459 tons of bombs
on enemy targets, more than any other group, including those
operational before the Kimbolton outfit. The 379th Bomb Group
led the 8th Air Force in bombing accuracy and was credited with
more sorties than any other bomb group. It also had the lowest
loss and abort rate of any unit in the 8th Air Force for an
extended period. The Group lost 149 B-17s in action. One B-17G,

Ole Gappy, completed 157 missions; this was probably more than any other 8th Air Force bomber.

Post-war, Kimbolton airfield reverted to RAF occupancy and it was finally sold off during 1960–64 when part of the old base was acquired by the former owner, the Duke of Manchester, and the remainder by public auction. The airfield was returned to agricultural use and the runways were torn up to make way for the Stow Longa Trading Estate.

Molesworth (Station 107), Huntingdonshire, now Cambridgeshire

One of the clutch of airfields in the area laid down for 8 Group RAF, Molesworth's first occupants were 460 Squadron, RAAF, with Wellington IV bombers on 15 November 1940. The Australians left in early January 1942 and were replaced by 159 Squadron with Liberators, but this unit left for Fayid, Egypt, in February 1942. Molesworth then had all its runways extended to the updated Class A specification for heavy bombers, the main one being 2000 yards long. Also, the original thirty-six hardstands were increased to fifty and two T2s and a J-type hangar were erected adjacent to the technical site. In June 1942 the 15th Bomb Squadron equipped with DB-7 medium bombers arrived. Operating from RAF Swanton Morley in Norfolk on 4 July, six of its crews flew the first American raid from the UK during World War II when they joined six 226 Squadron RAF crews in an attack on four airfields in Holland. The 15th Bomb Squadron remained at Molesworth until 11 September when it left to make way for the 303rd Bombardment Group (Heavy) with B-17 Fortresses. This Group, which became known as 'Hell's Angels', flew 364 bombing missions from 17 November 1942 to 25 April 1945, losing 165 Fortresses. It took part in the 8th Air Force's first heavy bomber raid on Germany on 27 January 1943 and was the first group in the 8th Air Force to fly 300 missions. It flew more operational sorties (10,721) than any other B-17 group in the 8th Air Force and dropped the second highest bomb tonnage (24,918 tons). Two of its airmen were awarded the Medal of Honor: 1/Lieutenant Jack W. Mathis on 18 March 1943 over Vegesack, Germany, and Technical Sergeant Forrest L. Vosler on 20 December 1943 over Bremen, Germany. The 303rd Bomb Group led the 1st Bomb Division on the Oschersleben raid of 11 January 1944 and lost ten B-17s. The Distinguished Unit Citation went to all 1st Bomb Division groups for this mission.

During the war years additional living sites were constructed north and south of the flying field on its eastern side to provide

B-17 41-24587 *Bad Check* at dispersal beside a cornfield at Molesworth in August 1943. On 11 January 1944 *Bad Check* was one of ten B-17s of the 303rd Bomb Group lost on the mission to Oschersleben, when all the 1st Bomb Division groups were awarded a Distinguished Unit Citation. Four men in Lieutenant George S. McClellan's crew were KIA and six taken into captivity. *(USAF)*

B-17F 41-24577 *Hell's Angels* of the 358th Bomb Squadron, 303rd Bomb Group, was the first heavy bomber to complete an 8th Air Force tour of twenty-five missions, between 16 October 1942 and 14 May 1943. After flying forty-eight missions, all without an abort, 41-24577 was flown back to the USA on 10 February 1944, having been autographed by hundreds of members of the 303rd Bomb Group at Molesworth.

Once back home, it joined up with its original pilot, Captain Ira Baldwin, for a War Bond tour of industrial war plants. When in 1942 Captain Ira E. Baldwin and his crew had picked up 41-24577, a new Boeing built B-17F from the United Airlines modification centre in Cheyenne, Wyoming, he had proposed the name 'YAKIMA QUEEN' after his hometown of Yakima in Washington state. The crew was not enthusiastic about the name and on or about their fourth mission Baldwin called the crew on the aircraft's intercom and asked, 'How about Hell's Angels?' after the World War I movie. Baldwin had been deeply impressed by the movie and 'Lilac Time'. The entire crew agreed. *Hell's Angels* and the crew must have had charmed lives. When they finished their twenty-five missions, the 303rd Bomb Group had only eight of the original thirty-five crews and B-17s left. In June 1943 when Baldwin was awaiting orders returning him to the USA, he was invited to a party at the Bovingdon Officers' Club. There, he met Ben Lyons who was assigned to the BBC in London. Lyons asked Baldwin how it was that he happened to name his plane *Hell's Angels*. Baldwin relayed the story to him, at which point he said, 'Did you know that I was the leading man in that picture?' Feeling somewhat embarrassed, Baldwin said, 'I guess I was too young to remember.' Ben Lyons then asked if he remembered the leading lady, Jean Harlow. Baldwin said 'I think I remember her.'

B-17G 42-102453 *Princess Pat* in the 358th Bomb Squadron, 303rd
Bomb Group, nosed over at Molesworth on 25 July 1944 when
2/Lieutenant O. B. Larson was flying it. The chin turret stoved in and
three of the propeller units suffered shock damage, but no one was
seriously injured. *(USAF)*

accommodation for a total of 2972 men. Howard E. Hernan, a
gunner in Claude Campbell's crew in the 359th Bomb Squadron,
recalls that base life was spartan to say the least.

> The combat crews were kept separate from the rest of the
> base personnel and we lived primarily in the NE corner of
> the Molesworth base in small Nissen huts with 12 men to a
> hut, making two crews. Most generally, right next door
> lived eight officers, which formed the rest of the two crews.
> We had a little coke stove but toilet facilities were a little
> lacking. We had a couple of flush toilets but no facilities to
> take a shower, so we rigged up a couple of barrels with a
> charcoal stove underneath to get a little warm water. A
> dirty body at high altitude was so much harder to keep
> warm and it always surprised me that better washing
> facilities for the combat crews were never provided.
>   At the first opportunity we ventured into Thrapston to
> buy some bicycles. I purchased a little sports model with
> 24-inch wheels for £5 and used it for cycling around the
> base, into Thrapston and for trips to buy fresh eggs.

Technical Sergeant John A. Dougherty, the engineer in Pense's crew who shared our hut, purchased a 26-inch wheel bike. His had more speed but mine had more power so we hooked them together. It was the most contrary thing to ride but we made many trips on it. When he was shot down I dismantled the tandem. I vowed there and then that whatever crew replaced Pense's I was not going to make friends. I would be sociable and as pleasant as I could, but it was too hard when you lost them. Even to this day I cannot remember who moved into the hut or even what they looked like.

What a life. Up at 1400 hours and the only sleep we got was in the afternoons and also, we were only getting two meals a day. There always seemed an abundance of sprouts. Combat crews were entitled to bacon and fried eggs on the morning of a mission, but there were not enough to go around. Sometimes we had powdered eggs and if they had been prepared right you couldn't tell the difference.

Post-war mural in a school building at Molesworth in October 1975.
(*Steve Gotts*)

Close up of the post-war mural in a school building at Molesworth in October 1975. *(Steve Gotts)*

Ben Smith, a radio operator in the 360th Bomb Squadron, would agree.

> We would don our flying coveralls, heated suits and boots and head to the Mess Hall down the road where the cooks were putting on a mission breakfast. The chefs were very solicitous – seemingly jovial. We could have pancakes, eggs sunny side up, or any way we wanted them. Sort of like, 'It's your last meal – you can have what you want'. To me it seemed a somewhat macabre occasion and I found their jollity very disquieting and out of place. I could eat none of the breakfast anyway. Even to this day I have butterflies before breakfast.
>
> If we wanted to take a shower on the base we had to go about half a mile to the showers. There was never any hot water. It was just too much trouble and a very punishing experience, so nobody bothered. Sponge baths had to do. After a time we couldn't smell ourselves; or we thought we smelled all right, because everybody smelled that way! We

never wore uniforms on base. I can recall wearing my flight coveralls for days at a time without taking them off. I would sleep in them too. We cleaned our ODs (wool uniforms) in aviation gas. Consequently, we smelled like gasoline when we dressed to go on pass.

All of the crews, officers and non-commissioned officers, were briefed together. The radio operators were also given a separate briefing, at which time they received a canvas packet with coded data in it called a 'flimsy'. In the main briefing hall, the target remained covered until the Intelligence Officer came in. He was a dapper individual, sporting a moustache and quite hearty in manner – for a good reason: he didn't have to go. These Intelligence Officers were non-flying personnel with some useful information and a lot more that was useless. His first move was to peel back the cover from the map, which act was always met with a loud groan from the assembled crews. They were a lively bunch, and time had to be allowed for them to get over the initial shock, sound off, and cuss a little while. After a time they subsided and he began. [On one occasion] We could see that the red lines pinned on the map went deep into Germany. The target was the Heinkel plant at Oranienburg in the suburbs of Berlin. We were told we could expect heavy fighter opposition, with flak at the target described as 'intense'. In other words, the target was heavily defended. We could see from the diagram that we were flying 'Tall-end Charlie' in the high squadron. There would be a lead squadron and a high squadron.

Briefing over, we got up and started out. We climbed onto lorries and headed out for the hardstands where the Forts were parked. The ground crews swarmed over our B-17 getting it ready. The armourers were arming the bombs in the bomb bay. It was still pitch dark. We put our machine guns into their casings and attached the gun belts. When this was done, we went to the dispersal tent and lay down on the canvas cots, which were there for that purpose. We tried to log a little sack time before 'Start Engines'. The signal for this was a red flare from the control tower. These quiet moments in the dispersal tent were always the worst part of the mission for me. I was always inflicted with an unbearable sadness at this time. I can still hear the clanking coughs of the aircraft engines as they struggled manfully in the damp mist and then caught up.

Ben Smith remembers the area around Molesworth with affection.

I visited a lot of nearby towns and villages. Kimbolton was nearby and Thrapston, too. These picturesque villages with thatch-roofed cottages were a delight to me. I was fond of the dignified, sturdy villagers, who were friendly and hospitable once I learned a few 'ice breakers'. Our base was in a lovely section of England on the perimeter of what is usually referred to as the Midlands. The countryside was unbelievably green and rolling. Many stately groves of trees ringed the base, and I was fond of taking long walks and bicycle rides in the countryside. I loved this verdant country. Somehow, I had the feeling that I had been here in another life. I knew that my roots were here – that my people had all come from England in earlier times. Anyone with a passion for literature could not help being in love with this lovely pastoral land. Beginning with Mother Goose, this land had shaped my life from childhood on. I knew it intimately from my books. So I bicycled constantly over hill and down dale, rejoicing in the lush greenery of Huntingdonshire. The war seemed far away . . . Every foot of this land was steeped in history. Near our base there was an old Saxon church, St Swithin's. It was a thousand years old and still being used for worship. There were many such churches scattered throughout this part of England. The parish church in Kimbolton was registered in the Doomsday Book, the census ordered by William the Conqueror in 1085. Catherine of Aragon spent the final years of her exile in nearby Kimbolton Castle. This was the country of John Bunyan, the great Puritan preacher. He had preached in all of the glades and hamlets hereabouts and had written his great allegory *Pilgrim's Progress* in Bedford Gaol only a few miles away . . . I was quite taken

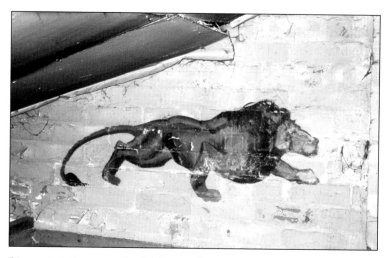

Lion painted on a wall at Molesworth in World War II, which was still in existence in October 1975. *(Steve Gotts)*

with the country inns and pubs and never intentionally passed one by. These were venerable institutions, nothing like saloons. They were homey places, family-oriented. Misbehavior was not tolerated in them. I eventually learned to appreciate the English ale and beer, served unchilled, and came to prefer them to the American, probably because they were much more potent. Their lager was phenomenally good. All of it had much more of a malt taste than our own.

Dick Johnson, co-pilot in 2/Lieutenant Theodore R. Beise's crew in the 303rd Bomb Group, arrived by bus at Molesworth in the last week of April 1944.

As we drove past the little village of Molesworth and turned onto the base, which was a little over a mile from that village, we were greeted with some strange sights. There were so many B-17s that they couldn't be easily counted. The 427th Squadron to which we had been assigned was on the base, while the other three squadrons

303rd Bomb Group mission log on a wall at Molesworth in 1975.
(*Steve Gotts*)

were just off the base. As we approached the barrack area of the 427th, some wag had hung a sign on the first billet area. The sign said, 'Girls who visit on a weekend must be off the base by Tuesday.' Along the taxiway near the armament section were row upon row of bombs out in the open. Some of these larger bombs were fitted with wings and empennage to be used as glide bombs. After we got settled in, and after hearing 'You'll be sorry' a few times, we did the latest schooling.

In July 1944 the 303rd Bomb Group became the first group in the 8th Air Force to complete 200 combat missions and was also the first to complete 300 missions, on 9 January 1945. Each time, according to tradition, the Group celebrated with parties. Ben Smith recalls:

We were stood down for three days. Military transport had brought in truckloads of whiskey and beer, including our favourite, lager. Invitations were sent out to all the neighbouring installations where females were stationed. Even the Land Army girls (female farm workers) were invited for those whose tastes ran to rusticity. They were a little odoriferous from their duties, it is true, but nothing that put them beyond the pale. So it began – non-stop drinking for days on end. The casualty lists mounted. The dispersal tents were booked solid. Bars were filled with wall-to-wall humanity, sodden and riotous. A visiting delegation of WCTU would have been dismayed at the terrible and unbelievable carnage wrought by alcohol. That it had corrupted young American manhood was indisputable, and here was the proof. There was a bit of extemporaneous nudity, especially among the females who knew that bacchanalian rites, such as we were observing, made this kind of costume imperative. Finally it was over; and what the Germans had not been able to do, alcohol had! The 303rd Bomb Group was completely out of business.

At the end of the war, Molesworth reverted to RAF control and operated in 12 Group, Fighter Command. Nos 441 and 442

Cruise missile bunkers at Molesworth, which were used by the 303rd Tactical Missile Wing from December 1986 to January 1989. *(Author)*

Squadrons of the Royal Canadian Air Force were based at the airfield during 1945–6 flying Mustang F3s. Other squadrons based at Molesworth at various times were: 124 'Baroda' Squadron flying Meteor IIIs; 226 OCU using DH103 Hornets; 19 Squadron with Spitfire 16s; 129 Squadron equipped with Spitfire IXs; 234 Squadron with Meteor IIIs and 54 Squadron with Tempest 2s.

The airfield closed in 1946 and was placed on a Care and Maintenance basis, but it was reopened in July 1951 for use by the USAF after enlargement, main runway extensions and modern facilities. Flying recommenced in February 1954 with the arrival of the USAF 582nd Air Resupply Group with B-29 Superfortresses, SA-16 Albatross search amphibian aircraft and C-47s and C-119 Flying Boxcar transports. In October 1956 the 582nd Air Resupply Group became the 42nd Troop Carrier Squadron and flew C-119 and C-54 Skymaster transports until December 1957. There was no further flying activity and the buildings and hangars were used only by USAF ground units for military storage and as a site for the auction of surplus stores. In 1973 the Nugent report recommended that 636 acres be disposed, subject to the retention of 115 acres for a USAF housing complex. From September 1985 to June 1988 more than fifty new facilities were built. A helicopter pad replaced the runways. In 1985 Molesworth hit the headlines when anti-nuclear campaigners occupied the site, which was eventually cleared and made ready for the arrival, in December 1986, of the 303rd Tactical Missile Wing with cruise missiles. The unit remained at Molesworth until 30 January 1989 when the base fell into disuse and it was lightly guarded. On 11 January 1990, it was announced that Molesworth was to be converted to accommodate an American military intelligence centre serving US forces and NATO and that some facilities would be modified to accommodate the wartime and exercise headquarters of the US Third Air Force. Construction work began in 1991 and was completed by 1995.

Nuthampstead (Station 131), Hertfordshire

Construction of Nuthampstead airfield started in 1942 in Scales Park on land owned by Baron Dimsdale, which lay three miles to the west of the A10 Hertford to Royston trunk road. The work was carried out by the 814th and 830th Engineer Battalions of the US Army. Station 131 was the nearest 8th Air Force bomber base to London, just thirty-five miles away, but it was one of the most isolated and the highest. During the construction of the airfield, rubble from the blitzed areas of London and Coventry was used for the foundations. The base was laid out to the standard bomber field specification with two T2 hangars and one main and two subsidiary runways. The utility and accommodation huts were sited to the west of the flying field and dispersed amongst farms and houses in the village of Nuthampstead. In September 1943 the 55th Fighter Group, equipped with Lockheed P-38H Lightnings, became the first American unit to occupy the base when it arrived to begin long-range escort missions for the bombers. The 55th Fighter Group flew its first combat mission on 15 October and thus became the first P-38 group of the 8th Air Force to see combat. Missions from Nuthampstead were dogged with problems with the Lightning's Allison engines, which were affected by the humidity and extreme cold at high altitudes over north-west Europe and resulted in a high rate of attrition. In March 1944 the Group's Lightnings became the first aircraft of the 8th Air Force to fly over Berlin. That same month the 55th Fighter Group moved to Wormingford to allow the B-17G Fortresses of the 398th Bomb Group to move in and become the third group in the 1st Combat Bomb Wing, whose two other bases were at Bassingbourn (91st Bomb Group) and Ridgewell (381st Bomb Group) nearby.

The air echelon began flying in from the US on 22 March and the 398th Bomb Group flew its first combat mission on 6 May. During the last twelve months of the war the Group flew 195 missions, taking part in raids on V-weapon sites in France and bombing targets that included Berlin, Munich, Kiel and

On 15 October 1944 a direct flak hit over Cologne, Germany, just after bombs away and the start of the turn away from the target, literally tore off the nose of B-17G 42-97746 piloted by 1/Lieutenant Lawrence M. deLancey of the 603rd Bomb Squadron, 398th Bomb Group. It instantly killed the togglier, Sergeant George Abbott. Without instruments and maps, 2/Lieutenant Raymond J. LeDoux, the navigator, managed to navigate the bomber back home, where deLancey and his co-pilot 1/Lieutenant Phillip H. Stahlman set the Fortress down at Nuthampstead without further mishap. The aircraft was salvaged later by the 2nd SAD. *(USAF)*

Munster. The 398th Bomb Group flew 6419 sorties and dropped 15,781.2 tons of bombs, losing fifty-eight Fortresses missing in action before being redeployed to the ZOI from May to June 1945. Nuthampstead airfield was transferred from the USAAF to RAF Maintenance Command on 10 July and used as an ordnance store by sub-sites of 94 and 95 MUs (Maintenance Units), until being reduced to inactive status on 30 October 1954. The airfield site was finally closed on 1 March 1959 and by 1960 had been returned to Baron Dimsdale, the former landowner, to become the Scales Park Estate. Almost all the runways and perimeter tracks were broken up and used as hardcore for the M1 motorway from London to Birmingham. In 1970 Nuthampstead was one of four sites put forward as a possible location for London's third airport (the others being Cublington, Foulness and another former 8th Air Force Base, Thurleigh). In January 1971 Nuthampstead was rejected.

Podington (Station 109), Bedfordshire

This airfield, almost completely surrounded by woodland, was built to accommodate RAF bombers, but in spring 1942 was one of several airfields made available to the 8th Air Force in England. The western end of the base had originally been the property of the Orlebar family, whose splendid old mansion, Hinwick House, stood on the road intersection just outside the gate. The eastern end of the aerodrome had originally been the property of Lord Luke. In September 1942 the 15th Bomb Squadron, equipped with Boston aircraft, arrived from Molesworth and remained until early November, when it began its movement to North Africa to support Operation *Torch*. From 18 August to 2 September 1942 some personnel of the 301st Bomb Group based at Chelveston also used the airfield. When the 301st Bomb Group also left for North Africa, expansion of the airfield began. The number of hardstandings was increased to fifty-two, but topographical limitations prevented attempts to lengthen the 1100-yard NW–SE runway.

From 2 to 8 June 1943 Podington was briefly used by the 100th Bomb Group, which was equipped with B-17 Fortresses, before the Group moved to Thorpe Abbots to join the 4th Bomb Wing. Podington was dormant again until 15 September when the

Nissen huts in the snow at Podington. *(Vie Pete Worby)*

92nd Bomb Group arrived by motor convoy from Alconbury to allow a new Pathfinder unit to be formed. The 92nd Bomb Group was nicknamed 'Fame's Favoured Few' and was the oldest group in the 8th Air Force, having been activated on 1 March 1942 at Barkesdale Field, Louisiana. However, the Group had flown just four combat missions during 1942, having been used mainly as a Combat Crew Replacement Centre at Bovingdon, from August 1942 to May 1943. The Group diarist wrote:

Podington was found to be in somewhat better condition than the Group's previous homes in England. The barracks were again Nissen huts or low frame buildings. The 92nd got settled in its new location in short order: roads and buildings were cleaned up; the process of adjusting to the new environment begun. Although Wellingborough was the nearest town into which a liberty run might be sent, it was also the home of a rather sizeable detachment of coloured troops and Northampton, about 18 miles away, was chosen. Bedford, the county seat of Bedfordshire, was slightly closer than Northampton but was being used as a recreational town for another Group. The Group's bicyclists however, rapidly discovered every village within a 15–20 mile radius and Wollaston, Podington, Rushden, Bozeat, Sharnbrook, Harrold and Olney among others, received the attentions of the GIs.

The 92nd Bomb Group flew its first mission from Podington on 23 September with an attack on Nantes in France. In October the Group took part in the costly raid on Schweinfurt and flew the 8th Air Force's longest mission on 9 October, to Gydnia, Poland. On 23 November the 92nd Bomb Group was alerted and briefed to perform the first scheduled raid on Berlin, but the mission was scrubbed before take-off. The Group's second Christmas in the ETO was celebrated in traditional fashion. Over 100 children from nearby villages, as well as crippled children from Hinwick Hall, were guests of the Group.

A Distinguished Unit Citation was awarded to the Group for its participation in the mission of 11 January 1944. On 20 May

Crumbling wartime huts at Podington in 1997. *(Mike Fuenfer)*

Partially restored wartime hut at Podington in 1997. *(Mike Fuenfer)*

1944 the 92nd Bomb Group suffered its second great disaster since losing nineteen men and twenty-one severely injured in a huge explosion at Alconbury during bombing up of a Fortress on 27 May 1943. Thirty-six B-17s were scheduled to take off. The high group was successfully airborne and at 0711 hours the lead group began taking off. Lieutenant Jack Pearl's aircraft crashed off the end of the runway. The next B-17 in line, piloted by 2/Lieutenant William W. Seitz, had begun its run, but it stopped approximately halfway down the runway, apparently having seen the red warning flares fired by the take-off controller and heard the radio order from control tower to stop take-off. Seitz turned his B-17 around and started back up the runway. The following ship in line, piloted by 1/Lieutenant James E. Wiggins, did not stop its run and the aircraft collided head-on and burst into flames. Five crewmembers escaped from each B-17 before the first of five terrific explosions began about three minutes after the collision. The final explosion was Pearl's ship. All aircraft were carrying six 1000-lb GP (General Purpose) bombs.

Medical personnel were in attendance at the time of the

crashes and when Pearl's ship careened off into the woods, the ambulance left the control tower and started around the perimeter track towards the scene. Due to the fog and the position of the aircraft deep in the woods, they had not located it at the time of the second crash. Directed there, the ambulance arrived at the time of the first explosion, suffering slight damage from flying debris. The ambulance picked up the five survivors of Seitz's crew. Eleven officers and nine enlisted men were killed outright and one officer died the following day. Nine EM were injured, some severely. Three Fortresses were destroyed and the runway was so badly damaged it required a platoon of the 831st Engineering Battalion (Avn) for three nights, in addition to the work of forty-five Air Ministry employees in the daytime, to restore the defective concrete sections and to resurface it with tarmac.

Another set of disasters befell the Group on Christmas Eve 1944. This was the day when the 8th Air Force mounted the largest single attack in its history, with over 2000 bombers participating in a direct tactical assault on the aerodromes in the Frankfurt area, and on road junctions, bridges and communications centres immediately behind the German bulge. The Field Order called for as many aircraft as the Group could put up and the 92nd Bomb Group dispatched fifty to bomb Giessen aerodrome near Frankfurt. The day's misfortunes started at take-off; the aircraft piloted by 2/Lieutenant Robert K. Seeber, a new pilot, took off in fog, which prevented a clear view of the trees about 200 yards to the left of the runway at its end. Seeber began to turn to get on course before much elevation was attained, encountered prop wash and, losing altitude, crashed into the treetops. The burning aircraft exploded about two minutes later. Due to the heavy fog and the position of the aircraft, deep in the woods known locally as Roberts Farm, it was not immediately located by the ambulances and crash crew. Six crewmembers were killed. Seeber and two others survived. 1/Lieutenant Charles H. Nesbit, Equipment Officer of the 325th Squadron, distinguished himself by his coolness and courage in carrying several crewmembers out of the wreckage, heedless of the possibility of further bomb explosions. Unfortunately, the three men rescued by Nesbit were too seriously injured to survive, even with the medical attention afforded them. On one occasion, Nesbit was within 100 feet of a bomb when it exploded and he miraculously escaped injury by dropping to the ground.

A serious fire in a Nissen hut used for pyrotechnics storage broke out at about 1400 hours and the Fire Fighting Platoon responded with every available man and full equipment. After moving two trucks loaded with flares from the side of the burning hut, the firemen attempted to extinguish the flames. After twenty minutes, with the fire gradually coming under control, the firemen were ordered away from the blaze because of the possibility of heavy explosions. An hour and a half later, with the danger of explosion apparently passed, the firemen were ordered to put out the blaze. The damage was estimated in the neighbourhood of $20,000.

The attack on the Giessen airfield cost the 92nd Bomb Group three B-17s missing in action. A fourth crash-landed at Lille and a fifth ploughed into the ground at Bury St Edmunds (Rougham), killing seven crewmembers outright and an eighth died of his injuries two days later.

William C. Stewart was a gunner in the 92nd Bomb Group, who arrived at Podington in January 1945, and he recalls:

The truck drove to the helmeted MPs [Military Police] at the main gate that opened in the link fence that protected the area. It was fairly flat countryside and we drove down the one main road of the base, past clustered areas on the left and right of wood and tarpaper barracks. Every so often there would be a painted sign that could be read from the road. One was, 'This Group flies the tightest formation in the ETO.' Another read, 'This Group takes no evasive action on the bomb run.'

I moved my gear into a barracks and threw it onto one of the lower bunks, which was conveniently near one of the two warm 'pot-bellied' stoves. One of the men said, 'You can take that bunk if you want but it belonged to our engineer, who got it through the head on a mission a couple of days ago.' With no further words I selected another bunk, farther away from the heat of the stove.

I was a fatalist at the time. I did not keep a diary. After my first mission I made a conscious decision not to write about what happened each day and the only record I kept was a listing of my missions. This I religiously tabulated on a sheet of paper I kept with my writing paper and letters from home. I thought that the odds against my making it through the 35 missions, required for a complete tour, were slim and I wouldn't really want my family or some Army personnel reading my inner secrets, should the inevitable occur. I was superstitious to the point that I would not go out in a mission without being sure that I had recorded the last one on the sheet. For some reason, I thought that if I did not do this, some dire consequence would take place. I was 19 and never really expected to make my 20th birthday, which was 28 May 1945.

In the final stages of the war, the 92nd Bomb Group experimented with British-designed 4500-lb 'Disney' bombs powered by a rocket motor in the tail, which were designed to

Men of the 92nd Bomb Group having a pint at the New Inn. (*Via Pete Worby*)

penetrate 20 feet of concrete. A trial was flown against the massive V-2 bunker at Watten in northern France, which had been captured by the Canadians. On 10 February 1945 nine B-17s, each with two *Disneys* under their wings, attacked E-boat pens at Ijmuiden, Holland, led by the 92nd Bomb Group Commander, Colonel James Wilson. One bomb scored a direct hit. Further trials were abandoned because the Low Countries were being overrun and targets in Norway were beyond the range of the Disney bombers.

'Fame's Favoured Few' flew a total of 308 combat missions and dropped 20,829.4 tons of bombs, losing 154 B-17s missing in action. The 92nd Bomb Group left Podington in July 1945 and the airfield was retained by the Air Ministry for storage. In 1961, Mr Ernie Braddock, a farmer, bought the airfield. In 1964 he was approached by a group of drag-racing enthusiasts who wanted to use the main runway as a drag strip and Santa Pod Raceway was born. The first race meeting was held at Easter 1966. In 1972, seven-eighths of a mile of the main runway was resurfaced and Santa Pod Raceway is now claimed to be the home of European Drag Racing. In summer 1990 Mr Braddick sold the entire airfield site to Anglo-Albion Investments Ltd of London. Part of the airfield (including Santa Pod Raceway) was taken over by a subsidiary company of Anglo-Albion entitled National Dragways Ltd, to be developed for other leisure activities.

Polebrook (Station 110), Northamptonshire

olebrook was the first airfield in the Northamptonshire–Huntingdonshire area to be built for RAF Bomber Command in late 1940/early 1941, by George Wimpey & Co. Ltd. A J-type hangar and two T2 hangars were erected on the northern side of the airfield. The longest runway was 1280 yards and there were thirty-six hardstandings, which made heavy bomber operation difficult. Nevertheless, 90 Squadron RAF arrived during 27–29 June 1941 with around a dozen Fortress I (B-17C) aircraft. The first of twenty Fortress Is had arrived on the Squadron in April 1941 and though the Americans suggested that they be used only for training until a more fully developed type was available, it was decided to modify them to operational standard. On 7 May 1941 90 Squadron was officially re-formed at Watton, Norfolk, under the command of 2 Group, whose headquarters was at Huntingdon. The squadron CO, Wing Commander J. MacDougall, or 'Mad Mac' as he was known, had previously commanded a Blenheim squadron. Limited flying was carried out at grass airfields at Bodney and Great Massingham in conditions that were far from ideal and Polebrook was little better. Much of the station was still under construction and the airfield tended to flood, while crews, used

Mission board at Polebrook in the 1950s. *(USAF)*

to pre-war built barracks at other aerodromes, found themselves billeted in wooden huts. On 8 July 90 Squadron flew the first RAF Fortress operation when three aircraft visited the docks at Wilhelmshaven. An attempt was made to bomb Berlin on 23 July, but all three Fortresses were thwarted by bad weather. Attempts to bomb the *Admiral von Scheer* in Oslo fiord in August and September 1941 failed and on 29 October four Fortress Is flew to the Middle East, leaving five at Polebrook to continue bombing operations. On 12 February 1942 90 Squadron was disbanded at Polebrook and a RAF Liberator conversion unit used Polebrook for a time. The two surviving Fortress Is were flown to India and later handed over to the USAAF. The RAF attempt at high-level daylight precision bombing had failed, but many lessons were learned about high-altitude flight and these led to improvements in oxygen supply, flying clothing and lubricants, while the Fortress design was subsequently improved with additional armour plating, self-sealing tanks and better armament.

Ironically, in the summer of 1942 Polebrook was turned over to the 8th Air Force and the next units to use the aerodrome were the 340th and 341st Bomb Squadrons of the 97th Bomb Group, which was equipped with the next Fortress model, the B-17E. This unit, whose two other bomb squadrons (342nd and 414th) decamped to the satellite airfield at Grafton Underwood, was the first USAAF heavy bomber organisation to arrive in Britain. In the meantime, Polebrook airfield was enlarged. The main runway was extended to 1950 yards and the other two runways were increased to 1400 yards, while the number of hardstandings was increased to fifty. An unusual feature was that the ammunition storage area was within the extended perimeter track. Dispersed living and communal sites were built in woodland to the north of the airfield and provided facilities for approximately 2900 men.

By mid-August 1942 the 97th Bomb Group had twenty-four crews ready for combat and the first American Fortress raid from Britain took place on 17 August. General Carl 'Tooey' Spaatz, the American air commander in Europe, and members of his staff attended the briefing at Grafton Underwood. At 1500 hours six B-17Es took off from Polebrook and flew a diversionary raid on St Omer. Briefing over at Grafton Underwood, the CO, Colonel Frank Armstrong, boarded *Butcher Shop*, which was piloted by Major Paul Tibbets, and led eleven B-17s to the marshalling yards at Rouen-Sotteville in north-western France. Spaatz had felt confident enough to allow General Ira C. Eaker to fly on the mission. He joined the crew of *Yankee Doodle*, lead aircraft of the second flight of six. Over the Channel, the Fortresses were joined by their RAF escort of Spitfire Vs. Visibility over the target was good and bombing was made from 23,000 feet. A few bombs hit a mile short of the target and one burst hit about a mile west in some woods, but the majority landed in the assigned area. Several repair and maintenance workshops were badly damaged, which put the railway temporarily out of action.

On 8 September the 342nd and 414th Bomb Squadrons joined the rest of the 97th Bomb Group at Polebrook. The Group flew the last of its fourteen missions from Polebrook on 21 October 1942, having lost four B-17s missing in action, and was removed from combat for transfer to the 12th Air Force in the Mediterranean theatre. Polebrook lay dormant until 12 April 1943 when the ground echelon of the 351st Bomb Group arrived and was joined by the air echelon three days later.

During the summer of 1943 Major Clark Gable the Hollywood movie star, who had won an Oscar for his role in *It Happened One Night* in 1934, was at Polebrook to make a different kind of movie. Although he was 42 years of age, on 12 August 1942, following the death of his actress wife Carole Lombard, who was killed in an air crash while on a Bond tour, Gable voluntarily enlisted in the USAAF. In October 1942 he graduated from the Officers' Candidate School in Miami as a second lieutenant and attended aerial gunnery school. On the personal insistence of General Hap Arnold, he was assigned to the 351st Bomb Group to make a motion picture of gunners in action. Gable's first flight was made from Molesworth in *Eight Ball Mk II* on a mission to Antwerp. Two more flights followed, to Villacoublay on 10 July and Gelsenkirchen on 12 August, much of the air-to-air film being taken by Gable and an MGM cameraman, Andrew J. McIntyre. On the next flight the Fortress *Ain't I Gruesome?* came under heavy attack and was hit fifteen times. Gable's last flight was on 23 September to Nantes. In October 1943, having accumulated more than 50,000 feet of 16-mm film, Gable returned to the US. *Combat America* finally appeared in October 1944.

On 10 November 1943 a Messerschmitt Bf 109F, a Junkers Ju 88A-4 and a Heinkel He 111H of 1426 (Enemy Aircraft) Flight from RAF Colly Weston arrived at Polebrook to provide a ground and flying demonstration. The Heinkel was originally from KG26 'Lion' *Geschwader* and had been shot down at Dalkeith, near Edinburgh, Scotland, on 9 February 1940, while raiding shipping in the Firth of Forth. It had crashed virtually intact. Coming in to land, the Ju 88 and the Heinkel approached from opposite ends of the same runway and to avoid a head-on collision the Heinkel pilot opened up his engines and climbed steeply to port. The He 111 stalled, spun in and exploded in flames, killing seven of the eleven people on board.

Lieutenant Joe Wroblewski, a pilot in the 509th Bomb Squadron, flew his second mission on 26 November 1943.

At 5:50 in the morning we were awakened for our second mission. For breakfast it was lousy grapefruit juice, powdered eggs, hard crisp bacon, dried up toast and all this mixed with plenty of powdered milk. On top of this hot cakes with syrup that tasted like molasses. Then coffee for the short-winded crewmembers. We could even go back for seconds if you could get by the firsts. After briefing for our mission to Bremen, Germany on where to expect flak and enemy fighters we were off. We had a hard time keeping up in formation, being 'tail-end Charlie!' The chin turret on *Shady Lady II* helped to multiply our problem of trying to hang in formation in a clumsy sluggish way. As a result we used up a considerable amount of fuel changing power settings continuously. At 27,600 feet the engines kept sputtering and gave us some trouble. Just about the time we reached enemy territory the tail-gunner's oxygen mask froze and he was without oxygen. Until another was brought back to him. The waist-gunner froze around his eyes and the ball-turret gunner froze his fingers. We were at 27,600 feet for 3 to 4 hours with a temperature of -55°C. Contrails were streaming behind each plane for a great distance. The black puffs of flak kept blossoming out on either side of us but not too close. They had our altitude figured very well. We had P-47 escort all the way and did not see any enemy fighters. Approximately 550 bombers were in the air for this mission. Due to cloud coverage and a solid overcast the pathfinder was used to locate the target. After dropping our bomb load our gas gauges showed only a little over 100 gallons in each tank. We all began to sweat. But as we started our descent with low power settings our perspiration disappeared. We had fuel to burn. Physically I was bushed.

The 351st Bomb Group remained at Polebrook until the end of the war and flew 311 combat missions, dropping just over 20,300 tons of bombs and losing 124 aircraft. It was awarded two Distinguished Unit Citations, the first for the 9 October 1943 raid on Anklam and the second for the mission on 11 January 1944. The 509th Bomb Squadron flew fifty-four consecutive missions without loss from June 1943 to January 1944. Two members of the 351st Bomb Group were awarded posthumous Medals of

Honor for their actions on 20 February 1944. During an attack by enemy fighters a cannon shell entered the cockpit of *Ten Horsepower* in the 510th Bomb Squadron, killing Flight Officer Ronald E. Bartley, the co-pilot, and rendering the pilot, 2/Lieutenant Clarence R. Nelson, unconscious. Sergeant Joseph F. Rex, the radio –operator, was also wounded in the attack and the bomber suffered severe damage. 2/Lieutenant Joseph R. Martin, the bombardier, decided that *Ten Horsepower* was finished and told the crew to bale out. Martin salvoed the bombs and then left the aircraft through the forward escape hatch. Sergeant Archie Mathies, the Scottish-born ball-turret gunner, and Sergeant Carl W. Moore, the top turret gunner-engineer, decided to see what could be done for the pilot. They clambered into the cockpit. 2/Lieutenant Walter E Truemper, the navigator, had also remained in the aircraft and went up front to help Mathies.

The windscreen was smashed but Mathies believed he could fly the bomber back to England. He and Truemper took it in turns to fly *Ten Horsepower*, while others struggled to remove the dead co-pilot from his seat and place him in the nose. Bartley's

B-17G-45-BO 42-97258 *Silver Meteor* of the 508th Bomb Squadron, 351st Bomb Group, which despite three crash-landings, survived the war only to be scrapped at Kingman, Arizona, in late 1945. *(USAF via Ron Mackay)*

limp body forced both men to crouch on the floor between the seats, using only the elevators and ailerons to keep the B-17 airborne. Mathies had the greater knowledge of how to fly a B-17 and completed most of the route home. At times the cold became so intense because of the smashed windscreen, that Truemper and the others had to take it in turns at the controls. Mathies and Truemper did not know how to land a B-17 so, when they reached Polebrook, Mathies called up the control tower and told them of their predicament. The crew was told to bale out over the airfield but Mathies and Truemper volunteered to remain aboard and try to bring the crippled bomber in for a crash-landing. Colonel Eugene A. Romig, the CO, Colonel Elzia Ledoux, the tower officer and a flight engineer took off in another B-17 with the intention of assisting in the landing by radioing instructions to Mathies. Unfortunately, radio contact could not be made between the two bombers and visual directions were impossible because *Ten Horsepower* was flying too erratically to allow Romig to get in closer. Romig decided the only course of action was for Mathies to fly the bomber towards the sea and bale out. Mathies and Truemper refused to leave their pilot and elected to try and land. The tower radioed a set of instructions and the now crowded flight line waited as Mathies came in for the first approach. *Ten Horsepower* was too high and he had to go around again. The second approach was also too high so Romig and Ledoux, via the tower at Polebrook, instructed Mathies and Truemper to head north and try to land at their home base. However, *Ten Horsepower* drifted north-east, passing Sawtry, the A1 road and Glatton airfield. Here, the B-17 drifted off to the left in a sweeping, diving turn past the control tower. Believing the crew was attempting to land, ground personnel fired off red flares. *Ten Horsepower* recrossed the A1 and headed towards the village of Denton, seven miles from RAF Upwood. Mathies and Truemper tried to put the B-17 down in a very large open field near Denton Hill just south of Stilton. *Ten Horsepower* was estimated to be travelling at 200 mph when it hit a mound of earth and then it cartwheeled before breaking into pieces. Mathies and Truemper died in the wreckage. Nelson was reportedly still alive when rescuers reached the wreckage, but he died later.

Polebrook also housed the headquarters of the 94th Combat Wing, which controlled the operations of the 351st and the 457th at Glatton and 401st at Deenethorpe. The 351st Bomb Group left Polebrook in July 1945 and the airfield reverted to RAF Maintenance Command on 10 July. No 273 MU (an aircraft storage unit) and 3 Ferry Pool were stationed there until late 1947. The station then became a satellite for RAF Upwood, before being declared inactive in October 1948. On 6 October 1958 the *Stars and Stripes* described Polebrook thus:

There's a 'GHOST American airfield' in England, just down the road from the modern US jet base at Alconbury, and it's fast becoming a favourite Yank tourist haunt. The installation – Polebrook, 60 miles north of London – was a beehive of activity during World War – when it served as the HQ of an American outfit. Today, it is as deserted as a haunted house. Jet age Yank airmen with a hankering to be transported back into history have only to visit there to get a hair-raising reminder of how things must have been there during the war. Some 50 buildings stand empty and deserted on the erstwhile busy base, their windows shattered and their doors creaking eerily on rusted hinges. Pigeons dart insanely about the bare interiors, with bats and field mice their only company. Inside the barracks, grass has forced its way up through the warped floorboards. Out by the runway, a tattered windsock still flutters above the old wartime flightline but has fallen prey to weeds. The roar of B-17s has long since gone. Polebrook, like many of the RAF bases hastily erected during the early World War Two days, has lain idle and uninhabited since the war. Everything remains just as it was left back at war's end in 1945, the huge hangars standing black and foreboding amid their silent surroundings and scores of old bomb shelters dot the landscape like rows of tombs. Strange, incongruous signs like 'Barbershop' and 'Chapel' dangle from the prefabricated huts here and there, but the sounds of snipping shears and hymnal voices have long been silent. In a huge building that apparently served as the officers' Mess, the ghosts virtually come alive as paintings

on the wall evoke memories of yesteryear. A sign over a
dusty counter identifies one room as the 'Oasis Bar' and the
insignia identifies the last tenant as the 351st BG. On the
walls are listed the raids the 351st participated in against
the Germans, along with the date and number of Nazi
aircraft destroyed. Names like Amiens and Hamburg and
Berlin are repeated often and alongside a Schweinfurt raid
on 17 August 1943 are painted 25 swastikas, one for each
Messerschmitt shot down. Another insignia of the 351st
hangs over the door – a golden eagle with bombs clutched
in its talons – and against the opposite wall is the familiar
emblem of the US 8th Air Force. The haunting atmosphere
of the abandoned B-17 base so excites the imagination of
some visitors that they swear they are able to detect the roar
of Flying Fortresses coming in for a landing – mission
completed.

In December 1959 a Thor ballistic missile squadron of Bomber
Command was formed at Polebrook and remained at the former
airfield until disbandment in August 1963. In 1964 preparations
for the sale of the airfield began and on 12 January 1967 the
Rothschild estate finally completed the purchase and
the runways and taxiways were broken up.

15

Ridgewell (Station 167), Essex

Ridgewell was one of the first stations completed to Class A heavy bomber airfield standard for the RAF. It was built in the parishes of Ridgewell, Ashen and Tilbury-juxta-Clare on a hill overlooking the Stour Valley and had dispersed living sites mainly in the parish of Tilbury-juxta-Clare on the southern side of the airfield. The airfield was opened on 29 December 1942 as a satellite to Stradishall in 3 Group RAF Bomber Command. First to arrive were Short Stirlings of 90 Squadron from Bottesford, which flew operations from the station until May 1943 when they moved to West Wickham. The airfield was enlarged to accommodate a large American influx, with the thirty-six existing hardstandings being increased to fifty and additional hutted accommodation being built to take a total of 421 officers and 2473 men. In June 1943 the Flying Fortresses of the 381st Bomb Group arrived from the USA and flew the first of 296 combat missions on 22 June, to Antwerp, Belgium. The last mission was flown on 25 April 1945, by which time the Group had lost 131 B-17s missing in action and dropped 22,159.5 tons of bombs on enemy targets. Its worst day was on 17 August 1943 when the Group lost eleven B-17s on the Schweinfurt raid, the highest losses of all groups that took part.

B-17Fs of the 381st Bomb Group at Ridgewell. *(USAF via Ron MacKay)*

B-17F 42-29751 *Mis-Abortion* of the 381st Bomb Group from Ridgewell in formation with other B-17s of the Group. This aircraft stalled on take-off on 31 March 1944 and crashed. *(USAF)*

The 381st Bomb Group was awarded the first of two Distinguished Unit Citations for its actions on the Bremen raid on 8 October 1943.

Two of the Group's most famous Fortresses were *Rotherhithe's Revenge*, for which savings certificates to the value of a Flying Fortress had been purchased by London's East-Enders. This B-17 completed over 100 missions, as did *Stage Door Canteen*, which was named in a special ceremony at Ridgewell on 23 April 1944 by Winston Churchill's daughter Mary, with the actress Vivian Leigh and other film personalities in attendance. The 381st Bomb Group left Ridgewell in June 1945 to return to the USA and on 15 July 1945 the airfield passed to RAF Maintenance Command with 94 MU, stationed here from 10 September 1946 to 31 March 1957. Between March 1960 and 1967 Ridgewell was used as a USAF off-base storage annex to RAF Wethersfield.

Thurleigh (Station 111), Bedfordshire

Thurleigh airfield was built originally for RAF Bomber Command by W. & C. French Ltd and 160 Squadron was formed at the station on 16 January 1942 as a Liberator bomber unit prior to imminent departure for Karachi, India. American bombers were awaited and during 1942–3 the runways were extended and additional hardstands laid while sixteen living and communal sites were dispersed in countryside to the east of the airfield and to the north of the village of Thurleigh. The bomb dump was situated in woodland to the north-west, while the technical site on the east of the airfield was unusual in having four hangars. The 306th Bomb Group arrived in September 1942 and remained at the base until December 1945. Not only was this the longest tenure by any American combat unit of a UK base during World War II, this base was also in continuous combat use longer than any other.

The 306th Bomb Group, whose first commander was Colonel Charles B. 'Chip' Overacker, flew its first combat mission on 9 October 1942. During its three years at Thurleigh, the 306th Bomb Group was visited by many VIPs, including King George VI and Queen Elizabeth and the then Princess Elizabeth, when she named a B-17 *Rose of York*.

HM King George VI and HRH Princess Elizabeth at Thurleigh on 6 July 1944, when she christened B-17G 42-102547, a lead ship in the 367th Bomb Squadron, *Rose of York*. Originally, the Fortress had been named *The Princess* by Master Sergeant Edward S. Gregory, its crew chief. Later, the name was changed to *Princess Elizabeth* and it was then that Gregory had the idea of having the plane christened by the Princess herself. The royal family agreed, but insisted that the name be changed because if it was shot down, it would present the Germans with a propaganda coup. Sergeant Malcolm B. Currie duly went ahead and painted the new insignia on the nose. At 12.30 pm prompt, a fifty-four-ship formation flew over the airfield in salute and, after the customary anthems and speeches, the Princess blessed the ship by breaking a bottle of English cider against a metal plate attached to the lowered guns of the chin turret. Captain Perry E. Raster's crew was presented to the royal family. *Rose of York*, flown by 1/Lieutenant Vernon E Daley Jr, was lost in the North Sea on 3 February 1945, returning from Berlin. All the crew perished. Also on board was Guy E. Byam, a war correspondent for the BBC, who had covered the D-Day landings and had jumped with the British Airborne at Arnhem. Staff Sergeant George G. Roberts was in hospital having his appendix removed at the time of the loss. *(Richards Collection)*

Words of a 306th Bomb
Group airman on a wall
at Thurleigh in 1994.
(Author)

One of the earliest visitors, on 14 November 1942, was
General Ira C. Eaker, chief of VIII Bomber Command, who was
far from impressed. The Group appeared 'slovenly and undisci-
plined' and there was a 'notable absence of spit and polish'. By
November 1942 the base was fast becoming the home of an
'unlucky' outfit. Losses were affecting morale, respiratory
ailments were rife and the enlisted men grumbled about un-
sanitary conditions and the poor food on offer. The 367th Bomb
Squadron was even known as the Clay Pigeons Squadron, the
nickname originating from an American war correspondent
who, writing in *The Saturday Evening Post*, said that the squadron
reminded him of a bunch of clay pigeons. (Between October
1942 and August 1943 the 367th Bomb Squadron suffered the
heaviest losses in VIII Bomber Command.) On 25 November,
the 306th Bomb Group was removed from the battle order, only

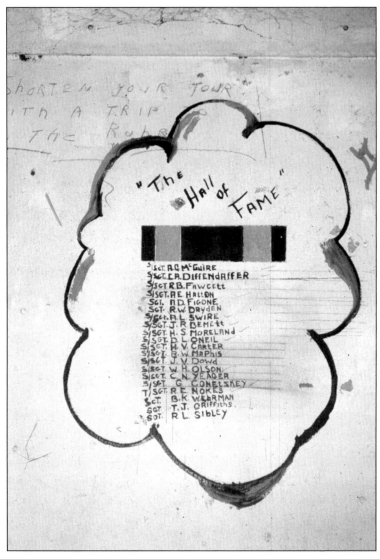

'Hall of fame' graffiti on a wall at Thurleigh in July 1973. *(Steve Gotts)*

Belle of the Blue of the 423rd Bomb Squadron, 306th Bomb Group, at Thurleigh on 20 July 1944 after a mission to Frankfurt. *Belle of the Blue* failed to return with 2/Lieutenant Daniel W. Gates' crew on the 12 September 1944 mission to Ruhland. The ball turret gunner was killed by fighters. The rest of the crew managed to bale out safely. *(via Richards)*

resuming combat missions again on 12 December. During another visit to Thurleigh on 4 January, at the main gate General Eaker's staff car was waved through without the necessary military courtesies and as he toured the base, lack of discipline and low morale were evident everywhere. Eaker finally sacked Overacker and on 4 January 1943 Colonel Frank A. Armstrong Jr, a West Pointer, was put in command of the 306th Bomb Group. One of Eaker's original staff officers, Armstrong had left VIII Bomber Command HQ in July 1942 to take command of the 97th Bomb Group after Cornelius Cousland was sacked. Armstrong led the 97th Bomb Group on the first all-American bombing raid of the European war and he and his 306th Bomb

Pin-up on wall at Thurleigh. *(Author)*

Poster advertising the 1949 movie classic *Twelve O'Clock High*, which owes much to the early events that were experienced by the 306th Bomb Group at Thurleigh. The fictionalised 918th Bomb Group was created by writer Beirne Lay, Jr, who arrived at the number by taking the 306th Bomb Group and multiplying it by three. Also, 'General Frank Savage' (played by Gregory Peck), the commander and the movie's central character, was modelled on Brigadier General Frank A. Armstrong Jr, who had commanded the Group for a time. *(Author)*

Group were selected by Eaker to lead the first American bombers over Germany on 27 January 1943.

The pulsating storyline in the literary and movie classic *Twelve O'Clock High* owes much to the early events that were experienced by the 306th Bomb Group at Thurleigh. The fictionalised 918th Bomb Group was created by writer Beirne Lay, Jr, who arrived at the number by taking the 306th Bomb Group and multiplying it by three. Also, 'General Frank Savage', the commander and the movie's central character, was modelled on Brigadier General Frank A. Armstrong Jr, with whom Bartlett

Traditional 'smoking' of the ceiling of the 306th Bomb Group Officers' Club at Thurleigh with missions. Major Harry Holt, CO 367th Bomb Squadron, until 4 March 1943 (left); Captain John L. Ryan (with candle); Captain John L. Lambert, 367th Bomb Squadron, later CO 423rd Bomb Squadron, and Captain George Buckey 367th Bomb Squadron CO, 19 August 1943 to 2 May 1944, lend support. Ryan took command of the 367th Bomb Squadron on 5 March, and was shot down the next day. He evaded and returned to England after forty-two days. This scene was used later in the famous movie *Twelve O'Clock High*. The 367th Bomb Squadron, which suffered the heaviest losses in 8th Bomber Command from October 1942 to August 1943, was nicknamed The Clay Pigeons. *(Richards Collection)*

B-17F-45-DL 42-3301 *Cavalier* of the 367th Bomb Squadron, 306th
Bomb Group, which bellied in at Thurleigh on 15 November 1943.
This Fortress was repaired, renamed *Bouncin' Baby*, and was salvaged
at Shipdham on 29 February 1944. *(Joseph Minton via Larry Goldstein)*

B-17F 42-30727 piloted by Lieutenant William C. Bisson in the 367th
Clay Pigeons Bomb Squadron, 306th Bomb Group, was one of ten
Fortresses the Thurleigh Group lost on 14 October 1943. Schweinfurt
was the target. Flak knocked out two of Bisson's engines, and fighters
riddled the rear fuselage, killing Staff Sergeant Thompson E. Wilson,
the tail gunner. Only 2/Lieutenant Chades R. Stafford, the co-pilot
(who exited through the side cockpit window), and four crewmen in
the aft section escaped death. *(Richards Collection)*

B-17G 43-38832/Y *Irene* of the 306th Bomb Group at Thurleigh with a
Disney bomb under its wing. *(USAF)*

had struck up a close friendship in World War II. In *Twelve O'Clock High* 'likable, decent, Colonel Keith Davenport' (modelled on Chip Overacker) is popular with his crews, but he cannot prevent the high losses, delegate, nor impose the strong discipline needed to change things. He is replaced by resolute hard taskmaster and West Pointer Frank Savage (modelled on Armstrong) played by Gregory Peck. Savage uncompromisingly sweeps into office not so much like a new broom, but like a whirlwind. Gradually, he earns his crew's grudging respect, but not their devotion. He does not seek it. He requires only their obedience instilled by military discipline, both in the air and on the ground. Training, training and more training follow, until the 918th's poor formation flying is improved.

Savage knows that wallowing in self pity and calling themselves the 'Hard Luck Group' is not going to help the aircrews, least of all place bombs squarely on target, the reason for their entire being. In what is arguably the most memorable scene in the movie, in the briefing room Savage finally brings the crews to the reality of their situation with swift, sharp, shock treatment. He stuns his new charges (and the audience) with a well-directed bucket of ice-cold water more accurate than a bomb strike. It chills every spine in the room, and in every theatre across the country. Savage fires from the hip and tells them straight, 'You're not going home. You're going to die. In fact, consider yourselves already dead!'

On 20 December 1942 at Thurleigh, home of the 367th Clay Pigeon
Squadron of the 306th Bomb Group, Maureen Easou, a three-year-old
Shirley Temple lookalike, accompanied by a Red Cross welfare
worker, visited the base to christen the popular Captain John L.
Ryan's B-17F 42-5130, *Sweet Pea*. Maureen lived in a London
orphanage and was adopted by the 367th Bomb Squadron as their
mascot after Corporal Irvin W. Combs (second from left) and fellow
enlisted men collected £101 (over $400) in silver and oversize English
pennies, enough to supply the extras for an English orphan for five
years. B-17F 42-5130, which had the words *Sweet Pea* stencilled on her
nose in anticipation of the christening, flew on the day's mission to
Romilly-sur-Seine, France. Ryan encountered strong fighter
opposition, however. He finally returned, on three engines and with a
large chunk of wing shot away, at around 3 o'clock, 2½ hours late to
keep his date with Maureen. Another B-17 had stood in, and someone
dabbed Maureen's fingers with red paint and pressed them onto one
of the plane's propeller blades so that the *Sweet Pea* could be
christened *in absentia*. Three months later, on 6 March 1943, the 'real'
Sweet Pea failed to return from the raid on Lorient. Ryan, the 367th
Squadron Commander elect, evaded capture, was rescued by the
French Underground and returned to England on 17 April, only forty-
two days after being shot down. *(Richards Collection)*

In the case of Frank Savage, we witness his steady mental decline as battle fatigue overtakes, and finally engulfs this remarkable leader of men. Ultimately, Savage allows the full weight of responsibility to fall squarely on his shoulders and his alone, much in the same way that events had overtaken Davenport. Savage continues to fly missions when it is not essential or required of him to do so. He insists on leading from the front as if he still has something to prove to his men. He begins to crack and then suffers the final painful mental breakdown at planeside prior to a mission. He is so wracked with mental fatigue that he cannot summon strength in his arms to lift himself up and into the nose of his B-17. This final part of Frank Savage's persona is not based on General Armstrong at all, but the incident, as Lay confirmed, did happen to 'a very fine commander'.

The movie begins in flashback with bespectacled Harvey Stovall (played by veteran screen and stage actor Dean Jagger) returning to his former base at Archbury where as a major he was the 918th Ground Executive. Stovall leans his bicycle against the wooden gate at the entrance to the disused and deserted wartime airfield and he surveys the overgrown dispersals where just a few years earlier, mighty Forts had stood. He squints across the English meadow where cows are grazing. In the wind Stovall can hear the roar of the engines and he and cinema-goers are cleverly transported back in time to the war when the 918th Bomb Group had dominated this now quiet pastoral scene. (*Twelve O'Clock High* was premiered at Grauman's Chinese Theatre in Hollywood on Christmas Day 1949.)

By April 1945 the 306th Bomb Group had flown 342 missions, dropping 22,574.6 tons of bombs and losing 171 B-17s missing in combat. There were successes and tragedies along the way. The Group had the first man in VIII Bomber Command to complete a tour when Technical Sergeant Michael K. Roscovitch, a gunner known as 'The Mad Russian', flew his twenty-fifth mission on 5 April 1943. The 369th Fightin' Bitin' Bomb Squadron flew forty-two consecutive missions without loss for over six months in 1943. Sergeant Maynard H. 'Snuffy' Smith Jr was awarded the Medal of Honor for actions that saved the B-17 in which he was a ball turret gunner, on his first mission on 1 May 1943. Two Distinguished Unit Citations were awarded, on 11 January 1944 (all 1st Bomb Division Groups) and on 22 February 1944 when the target was Bernberg.

After the war, Thurleigh airfield became the home of the Royal Aircraft Establishment experimental unit belonging to the Ministry of Defence, which obliterated much of the wartime airfield, hangars and other buildings and laid two new runways, one of them of great length.

Summary of the Airfields

ALCONBURY (STATION 102)/ABBOTS RIPTON (STATION 547) HUNTINGDONSHIRE, NOW CAMBRIDGESHIRE

Description: American bomber base used by the 92nd and 482nd Bomb Groups and the Radio Countermeasures Squadron in World War II.

Location: 5 miles NW of Huntingdon.

Comments: Little is left of Station 102 of World War II, though the 25-foot high earth shooting-in butt on the north side of the airfield is still a prominent landmark. The three wartime runways were replaced by a single 9000-foot runway, which served many types of aircraft. Outside the main entrance is an F-5E Aggressor 'gate guardian' aircraft. Now deactivated, the former base provides accommodation for USAF and associated civilian personnel.

In addition to being an operational bomber base, Alconbury also served as the flying field for the 2nd Strategic Air Depot at Abbots Ripton, which served the Fortress groups of the 1st Division as a major maintenance base. The site was constructed during 1943 on the eastern side of the airfield, mainly in the village of Little Stukeley. It comprised a looped taxiway off the perimeter track with twenty-four additional hardstandings. A technical complex of engineering workshops was adjacent to the site and beyond, to the south-east alongside the A14, were

Unit	From	To	Aircraft	Squadron Codes
92nd Bomb Group, 325th, 327th, 407th Bomb Squadrons	4–11 January 1943	11–16 September 1943	B-17E/F	NV UX PY
95th Bomb Group (air echelon only)	15 April 1943	15 June 1943	B-17E/F	(For combat training)
482nd Bomb Group, 812th, 813th, 814th Bomb Squadrons	20 August 1943	24 June 1945	B-17F/G B-24H/J/L/M	MI PC SI
Radio Countermeasures Squadron	28 February 1945	June 1945	B-17F/G (Jan–Sep 44). B-24H/J (June 44–May 45) P-51 (from late 44)	JJ/J6

several barracks and communal sites. The depot came into operation early in 1944 and was a completely independent station from Alconbury. It is claimed that on 15 December 1944 a UC-64 Norseman piloted by Flight Officer John Morgan left Abbots Ripton to pick up Glenn Miller at RAF Twinwoods for a flight to Paris, although no record of the departure in the control tower log nor any evidence of the flight has ever been produced.

BASSINGBOURN (STATION 121) CAMBRIDGESHIRE

Description: American bomber base used by the 401st and 91st Bomb Groups in World War II, the RAF post-war and, since 1969, a major British Army infantry training depot.
Location: 3½ miles N of Royston beside the A1198 (formerly the A14 and the old Roman road – 'Ermine Street').
Comments: In the late 1960s most of the runways were cleared, leaving only small sections for use by light military aircraft. With Army occupancy the hangars are used as indoor parade grounds. In front of a flagpole inside the main gate opposite the guardroom to the former airfield, which is now an Army barracks, is a B-17 propeller memorial. A stone bears the inscription: 'To honor all men of the 91st Bombardment Group (H) AAF Station 121 Bassingbourn Depot. American occupied 14 October 1942–23 June 1945. Never forgotten, forever honored.' The four

Squadrons of the 91st Bomb Group are also listed, together with all the ground support units. The memorial was unveiled on 23 May 1978. To commemorate the airfield's long association with the Canberra, which served here with 231 Operational Conversion Unit, a PR7, WJ821, is displayed within the camp. The wartime control tower has been turned into a memorial museum for both RAF and American units that were based at Bassingbourn. A section of the American display in the tower features the famed *Memphis Belle*. Visits to the control tower museum are best made at weekends or in the evenings. Intending visitors should first contact Mr Vince Hemmings, Curator, 48 Meadow Way, Letchworth, Hertfordshire SG6 3HX. Telephone: 01462 673340. The station pub is called 'The Memphis Belle' after the famous B-17 that flew from Bassingbourn. Some of the airfield's concrete has gone, but Bassingbourn's wartime control tower remains intact and is jealously cared for by the East Anglian Aviation Society, which has spent years converting it into a first-class museum, the ground floor being devoted to the RAF and the upper floor to the Americans. The building is packed with memorabilia and photographs.

A fountain dedicated to the memory of the 91st Bomb Group, paid for by donations from the Group's memorial association and the people of Royston, is in the park at Royston. Orwell church to the east retains its white face, which was painted to help crews see it more easily and avoid it. *See also Wimpole Hall.*

Unit	From	To	Aircraft	Squadron Codes
401st Bomb Group, 612th, 613th, 614th, 615th Bomb Squadrons (air echelon only)	Late October 1943	November 1943	B-17G	SC IN IW IY
91st Bomb Group, 322nd, 323rd, 324th, 401st Bomb Squadrons	14 October 1942	23 June 1945	B-17F/G	LG OR DF LL

BOVINGDON (STATION 112) HERTFORDSHIRE

Description: American bomber base used by the 92nd Bomb Group/CCRC in World War II.
Location: On the edge of the Chiltern Hills, 2 miles S of Berkhampstead and bordered on its southern boundary by the B4505 and Bovingdon village.
Comments: A few wartime buildings remain along a minor road at Whelpley Hill, west of the airfield site. There are two hardstands and a water tower. The big control tower stands derelict, between the earth and the prison fence.

Unit	From	To	Aircraft	Squadron Codes
92nd Bomb Group, 325th, 326th, 327th, 407th Bomb Squadrons	18–20 August 1942	4–11 January 1943	B-17E/F	NV JW UX PY

CHEDDINGTON (STATION 113) BUCKINGHAMSHIRE

Description: American bomber base used by the Night Leaflet and Radio Counter Measures Squadrons in World War II.
Location: On unclassified road 3 miles N of Tring and about 5 miles E of Aylesbury.
Directions: After Tring and New Mill Cross turn onto the B489, before turning right to Marsworth and left towards Long Marston. Look for sign saying Airfield Farm (SMS Farms Ltd). The memorial is at the right of the entrance near the road, at Gubblecote.

Unit	From	To	Aircraft	Squadron Codes
858th/406th Bomb Squadron (Night Leaflet Squadron)	24 June 1944	March 1945	B-17E/F and B-24H/J/M	JJ J6
Radio Counter Measures Squadron	14 August 1944	28 February 1945	B-17F/G, B-24H/J, P-51	

Comments: At the entrance to the old technical site is a memorial consisting of a runway light set in cobblestones and backed by a brick surround. A marble slab, surmounted by the 8th Air Force insignia, is inscribed: 'Dedicated October 1982 to the US 8th Army Air Force stationed here 1942–45.'

Chelveston (Station 105) Northamptonshire

Description: American bomber base used by the 301st and 305th Bomb Groups in World War II.
Location: On the south side of the A45, 6 miles E of Wellingborough.
Comments: Near the village of Caldecott-cum-Chelveston is the Parish Church of St John the Baptist. On the lower part of the thirteenth century church tower is a plaque with the inscription: 'This tower was restored with the help of the 305th Bombardment Group (H) Memorial Association. The Group was based at an airfield near this church from 1942 to 1945 during the World War II and consisted of four squadrons, the 422nd, 366th, 365th and 364th, plus attached units which flew B-17 Flying Fortress bombers as part of the Eighth Air Force of the Armed Forces of the United States America. This plaque was dedicated on 4th September 1980 in memory of more than 769 men killed and also those wounded during the 480 missions flown by Group.' The American veterans of the 305th Bomb Group provided a new sign for the church in late 1988 and the words 'American Memorial 305th Bomb Group 8th Air Force' appear at the bottom. Below the plaque is a memorial for Jane Recht who was the wife of Victor Recht, a waist gunner in the 305th Bomb Group. Near the church porch is a memorial seat for Marion Hoffman, wife of Dick Hoffman, top turret gunner on the same crew, known as the 'Stag Party'. The gravel drive from the road to the church was also paid for by subscriptions raised by the Americans.

In Sheffield, South Yorkshire, off the A625 2 miles SW of the city centre in Endcliffe Park, most easily reached by the Hunter's Bar entrance, is a plaque fixed to a large piece of rough quarried stone. It states: 'Erected by Sheffield RAF Association in memory of the ten crew of USAAF bomber which crashed in this park

22-2-1944. Per ardua ad astra. Air Crew John G. Krieghauser (Pilot), Lyle J. Curtis, John W. Humphrey, Melchor Hernandez, Robert E. Mayfield, Harry W. Estabrooks, Charles H. Tuttle, Maurice O. Robbins, Vito R. Ambrosio, George N. Williams.' Ten North American scarlet oaks are planted nearby, one for each of the men who died. The aircraft was B-17G 42-31322 *Mi Amigo* of the 305th Bomb Group and was returning from a diversionary raid on Aalborg, Denmark. First Lieutenant Krieghauser was awarded a posthumous DFC for avoiding houses in an attempt to force-land in the park.

Contact: Bill Donald, Arbury Cottage, 42 Harborough Road, Rushden NN10 0LP (Tel: 01933 359239).

Unit	From	To	Aircraft	Squadron Codes
301st Bomb Group, 32nd, 352nd, 353rd, 419th Bomb Squadrons	9 August 1942	8 December 1942	B-17F	None
305th Bomb Group, 364th, 365th, 366th, 422nd Bomb Squadrons	6–11 December 1942	20–26 July 1945	B-17F/G	WF XK KY JJ

DEENETHORPE (STATION 128) NORTHAMPTONSHIRE

Description: American bomber base used by the 401st Bomb Group in World War II.

Location: E of Corby on high ground south of Deenethorpe village.

Comments: Parts of the perimeter track, concrete tracks and footpaths remain. So, too, do some of the buildings, including the crumbling control tower, the operations room in the middle of a scrap car dump, the motor pool area, some mess halls and many small buildings. Near to the threshold of the former Runway 33 is an impressive granite memorial with a side view of a B-17 in bronze, as well as a plan of the three runways and perimeter track, which was made in the USA. The words on it are: 'To remember the 401st Bombardment Group H, 8th United States Army Air Force, Station 128–Deenethorpe, October 1943–June 1945. 612th Squadron, 613th Squadron, 614th

Squadron, 615th Squadron. From this airfield the gallant men of the 401st flew 254 combat missions over Germany and Occupied Europe in sturdy B-17 aircraft. The Group was awarded two Distinguished Unit Citations and had the best bombing accuracy record and second lowest loss ratio among B-17 Groups in the 8th Air Force. The best damned outfit in the USAAF. Dedicated September 1989. 401st Bombardment Group Association.' Some 120 veterans and their wives, headed by a former CO, Colonel William T. Seawell, who at 26 years of age was the youngest Group CO in the 8th Air Force, attended the dedication of the memorial on 16 September 1989. The old watch tower, which had the words 'Flying Control' in large letters over the upper windows, and which was used operationally for twenty-one months and stood derelict for about fifty years, was sold in 1963 and demolished in the mid 1990s as it was becoming unsafe. The underground Royal Observer Post, which was located just in front of the tower and was used as a lookout post for several years following the war, has also gone. Both hangars were dismantled, one being sold to Holland. The main runway was resurfaced for British Steel at Corby and used as a landing strip for executive jets. There is a propeller in the village hall from a 384th Bomb Group B-17 based at Grafton Underwood, which was on fire after a collision in fog with another B-17 and crashed trying to land at Deenethorpe.

See also The Wheatsheaf Hotel, Upper Benefield and The Church of St Mary the Virgin, Weldon.

Unit	From	To	Aircraft	Squadron Codes
401st Bomb Group, 612th, 613th, 614th, 615th Bomb Squadrons	3 November 1943	20 June 1945	B-17G	SC IN IW IY

Glatton (Conington) (Station 130), Huntingdonshire

Description: American bomber base used by the 457th Bomb Group in World War II.
Location: 11 miles N of Huntingdon and just S of Peterborough and to the E of the Al Great North Road.

The 457th Bomb Group memorial of a stone head of an airman, surmounting a plinth and looking towards Glatton aerodrome in the churchyard of All Saints Church, Conington (now redundant). The original memorial became weathered and difficult to repair and in 1982 it was reconstructed using Portland stone. *(GMS)*

Comments: Before leaving Glatton, a monument designed by Sergeant Lester Fried of the 457th Bomb Group was dedicated at a ceremony in the churchyard of All Saints Church, Conington (now redundant), on 30 May 1945. The memorial consists of a stone head of an airman, surmounting a plinth and looking towards Glatton aerodrome. Beneath it are the words of the 457th Bomb Group's motto 'Fail Accompli' and 'Lest we forget'. 'In perpetual memory of those valiant American airmen of the 457th Bomb Group H who, during World War II, gave their lives that freedom might prevail.' The original memorial became weathered and difficult to repair and in 1982 it was reconstructed using Portland stone.

One of the runways was partially removed and converted into a local road that runs between Conington and Holme and part of the perimeter track, along with the bomb dump, was completely removed. Sections of two runways were used by light aircraft at Peterborough Business Airfield. In 2000 the flying club was purchased by Aerolease from Klingair, the airfield operators, and renamed Flying Club Conington (Tel: 01487 834161).

Unit	From	To	Aircraft	Squadron Codes
457th Bomb Group, 748th, 749th, 750th, 751st Bomb Squadrons	21 January 1944	21 June 1945	B-17G	None

GRAFTON UNDERWOOD (STATION 106) NORTHAMPTONSHIRE

Description: American bomber base used by the 15th Bomb Squadron and 97th, 305th and 384th Bomb Groups in World War II.

Location: In well-wooded countryside, 3¾ miles NE of Kettering.

Comments: Although most of the concrete and buildings, which formed Station 106, are long gone, a few structures remain. The old HQ block still stands near road to Brigstock, intact but derelict. Briefing and debriefing buildings, two Quonset engine shops, the parachute building and three machine-gun nests survive on the airfield site, although crops may hide them. The woods, which sheltered the wartime domestic sites, have little trace of those days and are now used as an informal picnic area. The 384th Bomb Group's banner is in the village hall at Grafton Underwood.

On an unclassified road off the A43 on the threshold of what was once the main runway, is a granite memorial with the inscription: 'The 384th Bombardment Group (H) – 8th Air Force of the United States of America flew from this airfield 1943–1945.' On the reverse is: 'The first and last bombs dropped by the 8th Air Force were from aeroplanes flying from Grafton Underwood.' The badges of the Group's four squadrons and a B-17 motif at front and back are also represented. In 1984 this memorial replaced one unveiled on the old main runway on Sunday 25 September 1977 by 81-year-old William 'Pop' Dolan, which was beginning to crack and suffer from the effects of frost splitting. Although he was well over call-up age, Dolan, who was a fighter pilot in France with the American

Expeditionary Force in World War I, volunteered for active service in World War II and served as Group Combat Intelligence Officer at Grafton Underwood. On the airfield site behind the memorial are two avenues of trees, paid for by 384th Bomb Group veterans, which follow the outlines of two runways. One is called 'Budd Peaslee Avenue' after the Group's first CO, while the other is 'Pop Dolan Avenue'. The trees are 200 Wisconsin elms and planted amongst them are thirty-two other trees presented by the Daughters of the American Revolution and dedicated to 200 people killed when a USAF transport aircraft crashed on a Transatlantic flight during the 1980s.

In the church of St James the Apostle at Grafton Underwood is a stained glass window. It depicts a B-17 flying through a sky of deepening blues and shows the white cliffs of Dover, two white gulls and below them the message, 'Coming Home'. Standing in front of the window is a silver Celtic Cross and the Star of David, which represent the various religions of members of the Group. The cross was made and presented in 1988 by Clint Orean who was a 384th Bomb Group aircrew gunner, on one of his return visits to England. It is his personal tribute to fellow Americans who 'didn't make it back on missions'. Orean was shot down over Germany on his fifth mission in March 1944. Parachuting to safety, he landed in Belgium and was picked up by the Resistance, with whom he took part in blowing up rail communications after the invasion. Badges at the top of the window are of the squadrons, and the shield below that of the Group. The window was dedicated on 21 May 1983 by the Bishop of Peterborough in the presence of HRH Princess Alice, Duchess of Gloucester 'in remembrance of those who gave their lives for freedom during World War II while serving at Grafton Underwood 1942-45, especially those members of the 384th Bomb Group (H) of the United States 8th Air Force.'

Plaques beside the window were presented by members of the 384th Bomb Group. Two brass vases were presented by Georgina Daniels in memory of her brother, Captain Randy Jacobs, who was shot down and killed while flying as a pilot with the 384th Bomb Group. Veterans of the Group gave a big part of the cash and voluntarily subscribed for a major repair and maintenance project for the church costing £41,000, which began in April 1990. A plaque records the fact.

At St Andrew's Church, Great Cransley, 3 miles south-west of Kettering, serving members of the 384th Bomb Group gave the beautiful memorial window even before the war in Europe had ended. The idea for it arose when a group of airmen who flew from Grafton Underwood were returning from a Thanksgiving Day service at St Andrew's Church where many of them regularly worshipped. They talked of how much had been done to make them feel at home, and discussed how best they could make their thanksgiving. The donation of a window was suggested, but they soon found out that it would cost four times as much as they had estimated. Nevertheless, they pressed on with the idea, saved from their pay packets and raised the necessary sum. Now known as 'The American Window', it depicts in richly coloured glass 500 years of the story, which links Great Britain and the United States of America. The design includes the Archangel Michael of the Heavenly Hosts and the patron saint of airmen; John Cabot, the first English navigator, who sailed from Britain in 1497, and reached the New World; the Pilgrim Fathers; Thomas Hooker, the English Puritan who became minister of the first church of Cambridge, Massachusetts; William Penn, who drew up the frame of government for what became Pennsylvania; and Abraham Lincoln's Gettysburg address. In the tower the window brings history up to World War II and depicts the meeting between President Franklin Roosevelt and Prime Minister Winston Churchill. The window dedication took place on 6 May 1944. William Hoffenbacher and the Bishop of Peterborough gave addresses. Keys are available from the Vicar (Tel: 01536 791373).

Veterans and friends of the 384th Bomb Group have given a St Christopher statue and silver chalice to the Roman Catholic Church of St Edward, Kettering, and a St Christopher statue and bell to the parish church of St Peter and St Paul. The silver chalice was presented by 'Pop' Dolan.

Unit	From	To	Aircraft	Squadron Codes
15th Bomb Squadron	12 May 1942	8 June 1942	Douglas Boston III (DB-7)	
97th Bomb Group, 342nd & 414th Bomb Squadrons only	6 July 1942	To 12th Air Force XII BC 4 September 1942	B-17E/F	None
305th Bomb Group, 364th, 365th, 366th, 422nd Bomb Squadrons	12 September 1942	11 December 1942	B-17F	WF XK KY JJ
384th Bomb Group, 544th, 545th, 546th, 547th Bomb Squadrons	25 May 1943	16 June 1945	B-17F/G	SU JO BK SO

HARRINGTON (STATION 179) NORTHAMPTONSHIRE

Description: American bomber base used by the Carpetbaggers and the Night Leaflet Squadron in World War II.

Location: 5¼ miles W of Kettering and about 5 miles SE of Market Harborough.

Directions: Follow A508 from Northampton to Lamport and turn onto the B576 for the airfield site 2 miles distant.

Comments: The concrete pads for the Thors remain, as do some perimeter track and firing butts. Off an unclassified road 2 miles E of Kelmarsh at the east side of the B576 road (which was closed during the war to permit construction of the airfield), is a memorial to the 801st/492nd Bomb Group (H) Carpetbaggers. It is positioned on concrete near where two T2 hangars once stood. Veterans of 492nd Bomb Group raised £5000 in eleven months for the memorial, which was designed by an Englishman, Mr Ron Clark of Kettering, who during the war was an apprentice electrician working on the base. Aided by his wife, Mr Douglas D. Walker, an American who was a dispatcher with the 492nd Bomb Group during the war, recommended some refinements. Foxhall Cottages, on a side road off the B576, and the silhouette of a black Liberator taking off from Harrington, feature on the front face of the stone. Some Americans were billeted in the cottages and English ladies living there laundered items for

The memorial to the Carpetbaggers at Harrington. Foxhall Cottages, located on a side road off the B576, and the silhouette of a black Liberator taking off from Harrington feature on the front face of the stone. Some Americans were billeted in the cottages (in the centre of the photo in the distance) and English ladies living there laundered items for them. The memorial was dedicated at a ceremony attended by Group veterans and others on 19 September 1987. *(Author)*

them. The memorial was dedicated at a ceremony attended by Group veterans and others in driving rain on 19 September 1987. The words on the front of the stone read: 'The United States 8th Air Force 80lst/492nd Bombardment Group (H), Carpetbaggers, flew clandestine night missions from this secret airfield during World War Two in black B-24 Liberator bombers dropping munitions and supplies to underground resistance fighters in Nazi occupied Europe. They parachuted and landed OSS agents into Belgium, Denmark, France, The Netherlands, Norway and Germany to carry out espionage activities against enemy forces. They also flew night bombing missions. 208 American aircrewmen gave their lives flying from this airfield.' On the reverse of the memorial is a list of Harrington's supporting units.

Sixty memorial trees (red oaks, sycamores, maple and ash)

donated by local farmer John Hunt and his family were planted by the Americans during the visit at a site named 'Carpetbagger Cover' near the northern end of the main runway. The line of a new road, the Al–M1 link, cuts through the northern part of the site and passes within yards of the admin area of the former Station 179. It still has the brick-built admin building, which housed the commanding officer's office, the post office, map room and operations room. Now in it are stables, workshops and storage space. A nearby large Nissen hut was a canteen for officers (now storage) and the original flagpole is a few yards away. The bases of the hospital remain. In 1960 Bernard Tebbutt, a crop-spraying specialist and agricultural contractor, bought the site and laid water mains. Then he ran a nursery and built a large bungalow on the site of the briefing room, near the admin building, which became a museum for the Carpetbaggers (Tel: 01604 686608). Photographs and exhibits include the work of the SOE at Tempsford and the Cold War roles of the airfield at Harrington with Thor missiles and the Royal Observer Corps. Next door to the Carpetbagger Aviation Museum is the old paymaster general's Nissen hut, now the Northants Aviation Museum. It contains many remains of recovered World War II aircraft, including parts of a Lancaster, Hurricane, Tiger Moth, B-17 and a B-24. The exhibits also include instrumentation and other fascinating items of equipment and memorabilia.

Unit	From	To	Aircraft	Squadron Codes
492nd Bomb Group (Carpetbaggers)	28 March 1944	8 July 1945	B-24D/H/J C-47 Mosquito XVI A-26B	
406th Bomb Squadron (Night Leaflet Squadron)	March 1945	4 July 1945	B-17F/G B-24H/J	JJ J6

KIMBOLTON (STATION 117), HUNTINGDONSHIRE

Description: American bomber base used by the 91st and 379th Bomb Groups in World War II.
Location: West of St Neots off the A45 and B660 roads. The church is on the right at the western end of the main street.
Directions: Airfield site and memorial after Z-bend at the

Buxom beauty formerly
on a wall of the hospital
at Kimbolton. *(Bill Espie)*

western end of the main street on the B660. Bozeat Church is on
the eastern side of the road in the village on the A509 between
Newport Pagnell and Wellingborough.

Comments: Some perimeter track, some hardstands and a few
buildings and footings of one of the two T2 hangars remain.
Near the village of Stow Longa, at the Bicton Industrial Park, is
a memorial stone erected in August 1989 bearing the 8th Air
Force and 379th Bomb Group badges and the Triangle K
insignia. The inscription reads: 'Site of United States Army Air
Force Station 117, Kimbolton Airfield, 20th May 1943 to 4th July
1945. From this base the 379th Bombardment Group (Heavy), a
unit of the Eighth Air Force, flew 330 combat missions in the
B-17 "Flying Fortress" to destroy targets in Germany and
Occupied Europe during World War II. In memory of those who
served. Commanders Colonel Maurice A. Preston, November

1942 to October 1944. Colonel Lewis F. Lyle, October 1944 to May 1945.'

In the parish church at Kimbolton is a memorial stone for the 379th Bomb Group and below at the altar is a leather-bound memorial book produced by Sybil Smith, a local lady, in 1946. It lists the names of 353 Americans who lost their lives while stationed at the airfield. Ben Smith comments: 'In careful script the name and rank of each dead airman is entered on the pages of the book. Sad to say, the entries were many. These were the men of the 91st and 379th Heavy Bombardment Groups. These poignant instances underscore the nature of the Anglo-American relations far better than the trite phrase: "Overpaid, oversexed, and over here".'

A glass-fronted frame near the memorial stone contains a copy of the book *Shades of Kimbolton – a Narrative of the 379th Bombardment Group (H)* by Captain D. D. Robb, a member of the Group, which can be taken out and read. It is certified 'Book 4 of the second printing 1981'.

In the church at Bozeat is a card bearing an appreciative reply from Colonel Lewis E. Lyle, who commanded the Group for the last seven months of the war, to a message of gratitude from the villagers of Bozeat for the action of a pilot of the unit. In December 1944 he took off from Kimbolton on a mission but his B-17 got into trouble. All the crew except the captain baled out. It was reported that he stayed with the plane to avoid houses – and was killed. The church is locked, but the vicarage is nearby.

Unit	From	To	Aircraft	Squadron Codes
91st Bomb Group, 322nd, 323rd, 324th, 401st Bomb Squadrons	12 September 1942	13 October 1942	B-17F	LG OR DF LL
379th Bomb Group, 524th, 525th, 526th, 527th, Bomb Squadrons	20 May 1943	12 June 1945	B-17F/G	WA FR LF FO

MOLESWORTH (STATION 107) HUNTINGDONSHIRE, NOW CAMBRIDGESHIRE

Description: American bomber base used by the 15th Bomb Squadron and the 303rd Bomb Group in World War II.

Location: 10½ miles W of Huntingdon and N of the A604 Huntingdon to Kettering main road.

Directions: Driving from London, take the A1 road past St Neots and Buckden. Near Brampton take the A604 westbound towards Kettering. After 7 or 8 miles turn right into B660 and soon turn left into Brington, which has only one street. It peters out at the church. For the airfield site, see signs and follow B660.

Comments: All that remains of Station 107 are a much-modernised T2 and a J-type hangar and the old bomb dump. The J-hangar has served as a venue for several 8th Air Force-style 'Hangar Dances'. At the abandoned 'Peace Camp' site close to the main gate of RAF Molesworth is a cairn with a plaque reading: 'In commemoration of British and American servicemen who died from the indiscriminate use of chemicals and from nuclear tests.' Metal plaques at the airfield site commemorate the 303rd Bomb Group's two Medal of Honor winners, 1st Lieutenant Jack W. Mathis, in the doorway of the Headquarters Building, and Technical Sergeant Forrest L. Vosler, on the Mess Hall Building. The 'Hell's Angels' veterans association dedicated an impressive new polished granite memorial to the 303rd Bomb Group near the main gate entrance in June 2000. Part of the inscription says, 'They never turned back in the face of the enemy'.

In All Saints Church, Brington, between Huntingdon and Kettering off the B660, is a plaque inscribed: 'American servicemen stationed in this country made a gift of eighteen hundred pounds in 1958 towards the reconstruction of the spire of this church in memory of their fallen comrades and as a tribute to the hospitality extended to them by the people of Britain.' On 24 June 1984 a further plaque was dedicated to the 303rd Bomb Group, which once flew B-17s from Molesworth. It reads: 'In memory of members of the 303rd Bombardment Group (H) and its assigned support units, stationed at Molesworth, who gave their lives in the performance of their duties in the defense of the free world during the period of 12 September 1942–11 June 1945. Dedicated by 303rd Bomb Group Association June 1984.'

Unit	From	To	Aircraft	Squadron Codes
15th Bomb Squadron	8 June 1942	11 September 1942	Douglas Boston III (DB-7)	
303rd Bomb Group, 358th, 359th, 360th, 427th Bomb Squadrons	12 September 1942	11 June 1945	B-17F/G	VK BN PU GN

NUTHAMPSTEAD (STATION 131), HERTFORDSHIRE

Description: American fighter and bomber base used by the 398th Bomb Group in World War II.

Location: 3 miles W of the A10 Hertford to Royston trunk road.

Directions: Leave the M11 motorway at Junction 8 at Bishops Stortford and head W on A120, then onto A10 towards Royston to Barkway. Sign for minor road at right to Nuthampstead.

Comments: Most of the perimeter track and runways, the control tower and hangars are long gone, but a few small wartime buildings remain. On an unclassified road off the B1368 is the Woodman public house, which was close to the 602nd Bomb Squadron area. At the other side of the entrance to the Woodman, a large memorial stands on land donated by Robert Dimsdale to the 398th Bombardment Group (Heavy) Memorial Association under the auspices of the Nuthampstead Airfield Research Society. The top section is made of African ebony granite and has both sides engraved with a side elevation of a B-17, the constituent Squadron badges – the 600th, 601st, 602nd and 603rd – and the motto 'Hell From Heaven' with the unofficial Group insignia below. This represents the blue skies of heaven with fire coming from above. The two memorial base sections are of white Italian marble. The lower section forms the plinth and is unmarked. The higher section is engraved with the 8th Air Force insignia flanked by 1944 and 1945. A plaque at the left has the dedication for the memorial and includes all who served at Station 131. The other plaque lists the Group, the squadrons and the support units, the campaigns and battle honours and the countries against which their 195 missions were flown. At the rear is a plan view of the wartime airfield. The base lists the supporting units at Nuthampstead and the Group's campaigns in Europe. A further inscription reads: 'This memorial has been built by the 398th Bombardment Group (Heavy) Memorial Association under the auspices of the Nuthampstead Airfield Research Society. It is dedicated to the everlasting memory of those aircrews and support units who served so gallantly at Army Air Force Station 131 Nuthampstead-Hertfordshire-England. The 398th Bombardment Group (Heavy) flew 195 daylight combat missions from this airfield, losing 58 of their B-17G Flying Fortresses missing in action between May 6 1944–April 25 7945.' The memorial was dedicated on 21 September 1982 with sixty-six veterans and 300 local residents present. There is a memorial seat bearing the name of David Wells, who was 11 when the 398th Bomb Group arrived from the USA. In 1982 he became the local contact for the 398th Bomb Group and the old base. He died suddenly in 1989, aged 56. His son, Tim, took over as local contact and David's widow Peggy took an active interest in links with the Group.

In the Woodman pub 8th Air Force memorabilia, including a commemorative map of the airfield site above the fireplace in the large lounge, the Christmas dinner menu for 1944, a list of dates when the Union flag and the Stars and Stripes are to be flown over the memorial and photos can be viewed. The Friends of the 398th (Bomb Group) Memorial Association was formed in England in 1988 to provide a permanent contact with the 398th Bombardment Group (Heavy) Memorial Association of America, founded in 1978. On 11 June 2000 in St. Georges Church at Anstey a memorial stained glass window to the 398th was dedicated by the Bishop of St Albans and unveiled by HRH The Duke of Gloucester. The names of every man killed in action while serving with the 398th are etched into the window. A kneeling cushion in Anstey church is embroidered with the numbers of the four squadrons that flew from Nuthampstead.

Unit	From	To	Aircraft	Squadron Codes
398th Bomb Group, 600th, 601st, 602nd, 603rd Bomb Squadrons	22 April 1944	22 June 1945	B-17G	N8 3O K8 N7

Podington (Station 109), Bedfordshire

Description: American bomber base used by the 15th Bomb Squadron and 301st and 92nd Bomb Groups in World War II.

Location: 6 miles SE of Wellingborough.

Directions: Take the A509 road to Newport Pagnell, then the A422 and A509 through Olney to Wollaston. Turn right into Wollaston and take minor road for Podington. At T-junction see signs for Santa Pod and minor road to it across the road. For Podington and the Parish Church of St Mary the Virgin turn left at that T-junction. Wymington is further on, towards Rushden.

Comments: In 1972 seven-eighths of a mile of the main runway (one and a quarter miles long) was resurfaced for drag racing and used by Santa Pod Raceway. Many of the original buildings remain, including the two T2 hangars rented for storage, being occupied by various industries. In 1989 Mr Ernie Braddick, the owner of the airfield, converted the control tower into residential accommodation called 'Tower House'. In 1988 Mr Braddick donated a wall from the old 325th Bomb Squadron briefing/debriefing room with a painting of B-17G 43-38877/Q of the 325th Bomb Squadron flying through a flak-filled sky, dropping bombs, covering almost 36 square feet. The 1½ tons of brickwork was secured with a frame of steel girders and taken by articulated lorry to the IWM Museum at Duxford by the Eighth Wall Art Conservation Society (EWACS). Unfortunately, during 'restoration' by EWACS expert Heinz Bosowitz, the original mural was repainted, although the brick surround remained in its original condition, so any semblance of authenticity and uniqueness has been lost. Sergeant George Walschmidt, a 19-year-old ball turret gunner, completed the original painting in 1945 (43-38877/Q was assigned overseas on 9 February 1945).

The painting of B-17G 43-38877/Q of the 325th Bomb Squadron, 92nd
Bomb Group, flying through a flak-filled sky, dropping bombs, on a
wall of the 325th Bomb Squadron briefing/debriefing room at
Podington, before removal to the IWM Museum at Duxford in 1988.
Sergeant George Walschmidt, a 19-year old ball turret gunner,
completed the original painting, in 1945. *(Steve Gotts)*

Walschmidt died in 1988, only about 24 hours after the painting
was removed.

On an unclassified road off the A509, the organ in the church
bears the following inscription:

'In thanksgiving and in memory of Fame's Favoured Few the
92nd Bombardment Group of the United States 8th Air Force
1943–1945. In the cause of Peace and Freedom the Group flew
308 missions, 274 from Podington Airfield. This organ was
restored by the 92nd Bombardment Group Memorial
Corporation in the hope that the voice of this instrument will
speak for them – the living and the dead – to the people of
Podington every time it is played. Dedicated by John-Lord
Bishop of St Albans 18th May 1985.'

Beside the organ is a propeller blade mounted on a concrete
block.

The ties still bind. Ben Smith Jnr., a radio operator in the 303rd

Bomb Group, recalls an incident that shows the bond that bound the English and Americans together.

> In the summer of 1944, a young man named Staff Sergeant Bill Brockmeyer was flight engineer on a B-17 crew of the 92nd Bomb Group at Podington. On their first mission as they became airborne, they suddenly lost altitude and crashed into a wood at the end of the runway. A young farmer named Walter Nottage was working in the wood and ran to the crash site. There he saw Brockmeyer, the only survivor, walking around in the wreckage, dazed, his clothes on fire. Nottage dashed into the flames, scooped up the young American flier, and ran with him. He kept going until he was some distance from the crash, and luckily so; the bombs began to explode. In August 1977, through English friends in an association called Friends of the Eighth, we located Nottage! A group of us, Brockmeyer included, went over to see him. He had no idea what we wanted with him. Bill introduced himself, related the incident and told the now middle-aged Englishman that he was the living proof of this heroic feat. The two men, overcome with emotion, embraced and stood in silence for a long moment thinking of that fateful day in the long ago.

A stained glass window honouring the memory of those who served at Podington during World War II and donated and installed by the 92nd Bomb Group Memorial Association (UK), in the library at the Christopher Reeves Lower School, which overlooks Podington airfield, was dedicated on 8 July 2005. It shows a 'Triangle B' Flying Fortress heading for the continent on one of the 92nd Bomb Group's 303 combat missions, which is climbing to rendezvous with other 8th Air Force units in the cooperative effort of the USA and the UK as represented by their national flags. A plaque nearby acknowledges the many donations received from 92nd BGMA (UK) members in both the US and the UK and with particular gratitude for gifts made in honour of navigator Mel Engel, 327th Bomb Squadron, who had visited the school frequently in years past. The dedication was attended by Reverend Reed (who offered the dedication prayer), other church representatives, school staff and students, Podington area residents and forty members of the 92nd BGMA (UK), including twenty from the US, three of whom flew combat missions from Podington between 1943 and 1945. While visiting Podington the 92nd Bomb Group members dedicated a new road in Rushden named 'Liberty Way' in honour of all those who served in the area in World War II.

Unit	From	To	Aircraft	Squadron Codes
15th Bomb Squadron	11 September 1942	8 November 1942	Douglas Boston III (DB-7)	
301st Bomb Group, 352nd Bomb Squadron (Ground echelon only)	18 August 1942	2 September 1942	None	None
92nd Bomb Group, 325th, 326th, 327th, 407th Bomb Squadrons	11–15 September 1943	20 May–8 July 1945	B-17E/F/G YB-40 (May-July 43)	NV JW UX PY

Polebrook (Station 110), Northamptonshire

Description: American bomber base used by the 97th, 401st and 351st Bomb Groups in World War II.
Location: SSW of Oundle.
Directions: At Norman Cross, south of Peterborough, turn W on to a minor road through Folksworth and Lutton. Go towards Polebrook, but soon after Lutton see the sign at crossroads indicating a left turn there for the US memorial. (This is the Hemington road.) Go on this road then see a sign to turn right on to the airfield site for the memorial.
Comments: Only sections of the two runways and the J-hangar where an airfield visitors' book is kept, remain. (The two T2 hangars were burned down in 1979.) The control tower has been demolished, but an underground Royal Observer Corps post of post-war vintage remains derelict and flooded. Across the road from the old main entrance to the airfield in Ashton Woods are huts, which were used by ground personnel and are best reached from gateways on the Warmington road. The old ops block between the main entrance and the crossroads north-east

of the airfield is now empty. The north-east part of the site is the Ashton Estate's Nature Reserve. Thor missile pads remain. On an unclassified road 2 miles east of the village on concrete that was the north-east end of the main runway, is a triangular-shaped memorial dedicated on 18 June 1981. The inscription reads: 'In memory of the 351st Bombardment Group (Heavy) Eighth United States Army Air Force. 311 Group combat bombing missions were flown from this airfield over occupied Europe between 1943–1945. 175 B-17 Flying Fortresses and their crews were lost. 303 enemy aircraft were destroyed in aerial combat.' The badges of the 8th Air Force and the four Squadrons appear on the memorial, as well as a side elevation of a B-17. A separate stone shows a plan view of Polebrook aerodrome and is inscribed: 'USAAF Station 110 Polebrook. This monument and plaque stand on a section of the original main runway which extended 260° west from this point.' Nearby, in a box on a pole, is a visitors' book.

In the north transept of the Church of All Saints at Polebrook is a memorial containing the names of those who served on the airfield and other memorabilia, honour the 351st Bomb Group. A Stars and Stripes flag hangs from the wall inside. Keys are available from the Reverend (01832 274941) and Ann Richards (01832 273385).

Unit	From	To	Aircraft	Squadron Codes
97th Bomb Group HQ, 340th Bomb Squadron only	13 June 1942	25 November 1942	B-17E/F	None
401st Bomb Group, 612th, 613th, 614th, 615th, Bomb Squadrons (air echelon only)	Late October 1943	November 1943	B-17G	SC IN IW IY
351st Bomb Group, 508th, 509th, 510th, 511th Bomb Squadrons	15 April 1943	June 1945	B-17F/G	YB RU TU OS

RIDGEWELL (STATION 167), ESSEX

Description: American bomber base used by the 381st Bomb Group in World War II.

Location: Between the junction of the A604 Cambridge–Colchester road and the A1092 from Long Melford, on a hill overlooking the Stour Valley.

Comments: The site of Station 167 is now farmland, but most of the perimeter track and some runway remains, as do the two T2 hangars. Many Americans scratched their names in the concrete nearby. A section of the perimeter track is part of the Ashen–Yeldham road. At the east side of the main A604 road from Ridgewell village up a hill towards Great Yeldham on what was once the Station Sick Quarters site, is a memorial of polished black granite surmounted by the 'Triangle L' symbol of the 381st Bomb Group, beneath which is inscribed: '381st Bomb Group (Heavy) B 17, 8th Air Force USAAF, 532nd Bomb Sq. 533rd Bomb Sq, 534th Bomb Sq, 535th Bomb Sq and 432nd Air Service Group. Dedicated to the honor of those members who valiantly served and gallantly died in defense of Britain and the Free World against tyranny and oppression so that we all may live in peace and freedom with dignity.' The inscription on the left wing reads: 'First Mission 22 June 1943. Final Mission 25 April 1945. Total combat operations 297. Sorties 9035. Enemy fighters destroyed 223. Probables 40. Damaged 162. Over 22,000 tons of bombs dropped. Station 167 Ridgewell.' That on the right states: 'Let this memorial be an inspiration to the oppressed and a warning to would be aggressors that Peace is our ultimate goal. Further let it remind all former members of their proud heritage and give them renewed strength to meet the challenges of the future.'

Ridgewell Airfield Commemorative Museum, a private

Unit	From	To	Aircraft	Squadron Codes
381st Bomb Group, 532nd, 533rd, 534th, 535th Bomb Squadrons	31 May 1943	24 June 1945	B-17F/G	??/VE OQ/VP JZ/GD PL/MS

collection of USAAF and RAF items, behind the War memorial off the A 1017 between Rigewell and Great Yeldham. Tel. Tony Ince on 01787 476341 or Jim Tennet 01767 277310. Admission free. 2nd Sunday of each month, April–September 11.00 am–5.00 pm.

THURLEIGH (STATION 111), BEDFORDSHIRE

Description: American bomber base used by the 306th Bomb Group in World War II.

Location: 5 miles N of Bedford between the A6 and B660 roads.

Directions: From Bedford follow the A6 northbound. At Milton Ernest village turn right into Milton Road (signed 'Thurleigh').

Comments: An industrial site since the closure of the RAE facility in May 1994, a hangar and other dispersed buildings survive. One mile NE of the village at the former main gate of the RAE is a memorial to the 306th Bomb Group. A plaque in its centre says: 'In honor of air, ground and support personnel of Station 111 (US 8th Army Air Force). From this base during the years 1942–45 the 306th Bombardment Group (Heavy) carried out 341 daylight bombing missions against Fortress Europe. Some returned, others did not. All served and fought for freedom.' Other World War II buildings exist on the airfield, chief of which is the 306th Bomb Group Heritage Museum (Tel: 01234 708715).

See also Milton Ernest and Twinwood Farm.

Unit	From	To	Aircraft	Squadron Codes
306th Bomb Group, 367th, 368th, 369th, 423rd Bomb Squadrons	7 September 1942	15 December 1945	B-17F/G	GY BO WW RO

APPENDIX II

1st Air Divison Order of Battle

B-17 BOMB GROUP ASSIGNMENTS
VIII BC/1ST BOMB WING/1ST BOMB DIVISION/
1ST AIR DIVISION 1942-45

Group	Wing & Command Assignment	
97th Bomb Group	VIII BC	20/5/42
	1st BW	8/42
	(To 12th AF XII BC)	4/9/42)
301st Bomb Group	VIII BC	20/5/42
	1st BW	8/42
	(To 12th AF XII BC)	14/9/42)
91st Bomb Group	VIII BC, 1st BW	9/42
	101st PCBW	2/43
	1st CBW	13/9/43
92nd Bomb Group	VIII BC, 1st BW	8/42
	102nd PCBW	5/43
	40th CBW	13/9/43
303rd Bomb Group	VIII BC, 1st BW	10/9/42
	102nd PCBW	2/43
	103rd PCBW	5/43
	41st CBW	13/9/43

Group	Wing & Command Assignment	
305th Bomb Group	VIII BC, 1st BW	9/42
	102nd PCBW	2/43
	103rd PCBW	5/43
	41st CBW	13/9/43
306th Bomb Group	VIII BC, 1st BW	9/42
	101st PCBW	2/43
	102nd PCBW	6/43
	40th CBW	13/9/43
351st Bomb Group	101st PCBW	5/43
	1st CBW	13/9/43
	92nd CBW	1/11/43
	94th CBW	15/12/43
379th Bomb Group	103rd PCBW	5/43
	41st CBW	13/9/43
381st Bomb Group	101st PCBW	6/43
	1st CBW	13/9/43
384th Bomb Group	103rd PCBW	6/43
	41st CBW	13/9/43
398th Bomb Group	1st CBW	22/4/44
401st Bomb Group	92nd CBW	1/11/43
	94th CBW	15/12/43
457th Bomb Group	94th CBW	21/1/44
482nd Bomb Group	VIII BC, 1st BD	8/1/44
	VIII AFCC	14/2/44
	VIII FC	1 Oct 44
	1st AD	1 Jan 45
Night Leaflet Squadron	VIII BC, 1st BD	10/43
	VIII BC, 1st BD	1/44
	VIII AFCC	2/44
	1st AD	1/1/45
Radio Countermeasures Squadron	1st AD	1/1/45

Additional Places of Interest – the American Connection

Ampthill, Bedfordshire

Description: One of Bedfordshire's finest market towns, with picturesque narrow streets lined with attractive cottages and Georgian Houses.

Location: SSW of Bedford between the M1 and A6 on the A418.

Comments: As well as the market, which is held on Thursday, visitors will delight at the attractive antique and gift shops to be found in the town centre. The local parish church dates from the fourteenth century and is set back in a small quiet square. Inside are several brasses and a monument to Richard Nicholls, who was sent as a commissioner to oversee the surrender of Nieu Amsterdam (in 1664), which he then called New York, after the then King of England's brother, James, Duke of York. He eventually became the first Governor of Long Island.

BEDFORD

The county town was a bustling 'Liberty Town' for the thousands of troops and airmen stationed nearby who frequented the pubs and dance halls and the American Red Cross Officers' Club on the corner of Kimbolton Road and Goldington Road (now a car park). The ARC Enlisted Men's Club was on the corner of Union Street and Bromham Road (now private flats) and the ARC Club, which provided additional social premises was on the corner of Midland Road and River Street (now the Pilgrim Bar). In premises at Bromham Road, Anona Moeser of the American Red Cross established the first American Red Cross Club in England, which became part of the 'morale and recreation' programme for the young, homesick Yanks. Anona recruited local women to help her clean the dilapidated premises and once furnished, she advertised in *The Bedfordshire Times* for 'dancing girls' to visit the premises to partner 'her boys'. Bedford's mayor Alderman Canvin, who was convinced that the GIs came to England only to dance and woo the women,

Anona Moeser at the American Red Cross Club at Bromham Road in Bedford. *(Richards)*

severely criticised Anona for her bad taste in tying to encourage 'women of ill-repute' into the club. It was only after Lady Michael Bowes-Lyon, who was part of the volunteer kitchen-crew at the club, told her sister-in-law, the Queen, about all the fuss, that her Majesty herself paid the questionable club a visit and decided that the dancing-girl request was well justified.

> One day at the GI Club in Bedford a young flyer due to fly a mission the next day, asked me for a loan of £5 so he could go out on the town with his buddies that evening. He was so persuasive and I had such a strange feeling about this boy that against my better judgement and firm principles, I finally agreed and handed him the money. He left a small, green marble with me as security on the loan explaining that he had nothing else of any value in his possession. The next day he went down in his B-17 and the little green marble was left at the back of my desk drawer for the next few months. It was only when I was clearing my desk, ready for the move to Cherbourg, that a friend told me that the 'marble' was actually a rare piece of jade and was quite valuable. So I had it made up into a ring and I have worn it ever since in memory of that young boy and the thousands like him who lived for the day, for there might well be another one for them.

With the outbreak of World War II the BBC evacuated various departments from London to ensure regular broadcasting uninterrupted by German air raids on the capital. The Bunyan Meeting House in Church Buildings, Mill Street, was the BBC's Technical HQ for both the BBC's Music and Religious Departments and the AEF programme in which Glenn Miler contributed so much. On 9 July 1944 the Glenn Miller AEF band, which were billeted in the ARC Enlisted Men's Club and the annexe at 42/44 Ashburnham Road (Miller was billeted in the Red Cross Club from July to December 1944), made its first live broadcast from the Corn Exchange in St Paul's Square. Studio 1 was the major broadcast and concert venue for both Miller's AEF Band and the BBC Symphony Orchestra. Most of the concerts were open to the public and the auditorium was

The Corn Exchange in St Paul's Square, Bedford, where on 9 July 1944 the Glenn Miller AEF band, which was billeted in the town, made its first live broadcast. Studio 1 was the major broadcast and concert venue for both Miller's AEF band and the BBC Symphony Orchestra. Most of the concerts were open to the public and the auditorium was filled to overflowing with service personnel from nearby bases and camps. (*Author*)

filled to overflowing with service personnel from nearby bases and camps. The Co-Partners Hall off Havelock Street, Queen's Park, was known as Studio 4 and was used by the AEF band for rehearsals and broadcasting.

During his first twenty-four missions Lieutenant Richard 'Dick' Johnson, a pilot in the 303rd Bomb Group at Molesworth, had been to London twice for overnight passes, but he preferred going to Bedford.

In my High School at McLeansboro, Illinois, the book, *Pilgrim's Progress* was required reading. It was here in Bedford, England that the author, John Bunyan wrote this Christian anthology while he was in prison. I was impressed by this fact and was dismayed in 1992 to find that the prison had been torn down. John Bunyan was the rector of a large Church in Bedford. While visiting Bedford, I stayed overnight in the Red Cross billet there. One night as I was getting ready to go to bed, Glenn Miller and David Niven walked in to spend the night also. They both spoke to me briefly, and Glenn Miller asked me if I had caught their show. I told them that I didn't know about it. He said that they had just completed his first band concert in England. And I missed it. The Red Cross billet was in a large auditorium that had been partitioned off in eight-foot high walls to form two-man cubicles with an open top. I stayed in one cubicle by myself, and they shared the one next to me. They stayed awake for an hour or so telling each other the latest off-colour jokes. Many I hadn't heard. The next morning I got up early, since I seemed to be used to it. I was having breakfast when they walked in and asked me what was good. I told them what I was having, but didn't follow up on the conversation. My shyness kept me from even asking either of them for an autograph, because I didn't want to seem pushy. I never saw either of them again.

The thing that really caught my eye in Bedford, Cambridge and London was the incredible number of bicycles. The streets would be full of them as far as the eye could see in the late afternoon. At times it was difficult to find a place to cross the street. It was necessary to go to an intersection and wait for a Bobby to halt traffic before I could cross. Gasoline was strictly rationed and cost the equivalent of about four dollars a gallon. I found it incredible that we were burning about two million gallons of gas per mission, and I suppose the British were doing the same thing on their night raids.

BEDFORDSHIRE'S COVERT ACTIVITIES

It had quickly become apparent that Britain urgently needed to rebuild its contacts and intelligence networks on the Continent and give as much support as possible to resistance groups that were beginning to spring up in the occupied countries. Perhaps by accident or because of its central location amidst the airfields of East Anglia and its easy access to London, Bedfordshire became the focal point for secret counter measures against the enemy. Bedford became the centre of an intriguing triangle of wartime activity. Code breaking, radio surveillance, and the training and delivery of secret agents became a round-the-clock activity. Within a 30-mile radius of the town, there were so many sites and locations involved in covert operations, espionage and subterfuge, that one modern-day senior military official described Bedfordshire as the 'spy capital of Britain'. The organisation and control of such agents tested with two organisations – the British Special Operations Executive (SOE) and the American Office of Strategic Services (OSS). It is estimated that the SOE/OSS dispatched over 13,000 male and female agents to occupied Europe to organise resistance groups and destroy enemy installations, knowing that if they were captured, torture and execution would almost certainly follow. The listening station at RAF Chicksands, the decoding station at Bletchley Park and the airfields at Tempsford, Harrington and Cheddington all played their part in fighting the 'Secret War'. Further details can be obtained from Bedford Tourist Information Centre.

Even elements of the BBC's activities were shrouded in secrecy as it broadcast to the nation from its new secret location in Bedford as 'somewhere in England'. The BBC also contributed directly to the war effort by broadcasting coded messages in its normal programme output.

The Political Warfare Executive found its home for a while at Woburn Abbey and a Japanese language school was established in Bedford. Under Captain Oswald Tuck, the school occupied the premises above the gas showrooms at 2 The Broadway and later moved to De Parys Avenue. The school selected and trained decoding agents for Bletchley Park in a record six months! Winston Churchill said that the work done at Bletchley Park to break the German *Enigma* code shortened the war by as much as two years.

See also Milton Ernest and Twinwood Farm.

BRAMPTON GRANGE

Description: 1st Bomb/Air Division HQ.
Location: S of the A604 between Huntingdon and Winchingbrooke.
Comments: 1st Bomb/Air Division HQ throughout the war, now a hotel.

CAMBRIDGE

One of the most famous watering holes for American and Allied airmen in World War II was the Airman's Bar in the Eagle Public House in Benet Street. 'Smoked' on the ceiling are the names and numbers of American bomb groups and RAF squadrons, which were originally applied during the war years. Cambridge boasted six clubs, five for enlisted men and one for officers. G. M. Trevelyan 'one of the great historians of England', was available to meet GIs at the American Red Cross Club (Bull Hotel) in Trumpington Street every Saturday at 4 o'clock. In *Thoughts At*

The famous ceiling at the Eagle pub in Benet Street, Cambridge.
(Author)

Cambridge American serviceman Robert S. Arbib Jr, author of
Here We Are Together, said:

> Someone once said that the River Cam along the
> Cambridge 'backs' was the most beautiful half-mile in
> England. Standing now on the carpet of green lawn of
> King's College on that bright June afternoon, I was in no
> mood to disagree. Here, if anywhere in England, was a spot
> where tradition, architecture, history and landscape
> blended into a perfect, harmonious whole. Here was the
> past in the magnificent old chapel and the perfect classic
> proportion of the adjacent Clare; here was age and beauty.
> Here, too, overhead was the present, as British bombers
> wheeled and manoeuvred in the afternoon sunlight. Here,
> too, was the future, walking about the courtyard in the
> uniform of air cadets – talking from window to window
> across the court – lazing idly at the riverbank. Here all ages
> met.
>
> Cambridge University, if you excepted the sky above it,
> which invades all sanctuaries, was an island of peace and
> contemplation set in the stormy sea of war that swirled
> around Eastern England. The streets of the town were
> crowded with British airmen, WAAFs; farmers come to
> market, Americans who flocked to their club in the Bull
> Hotel. But once inside those massive iron gates, you left the
> noise and hurly-burly of the world outside; you entered a
> cloistered, ordered and somehow a remote world where
> every stone and every blade of grass cried out 'I belong
> here . . . just here!'

Near the end of his tour of missions Ben Smith, a radio operator in the 360th Bomb Squadron, 303rd Bomb Group, at
Molesworth, obtained a three-day pass and visited Cambridge.

> This lovely old university town . . . was only about twenty
> miles from our station. I fell in love with the place. Its fine
> old Gothic buildings, many of them dating from the thir-
> teenth and fourteenth centuries, were deeply satisfying to
> me. I could not get enough of roaming its medieval streets.

Everyone walked or rode bicycles; the streets were almost too winding and narrow for automobiles. Here the timbered veneers of Tudor England were very much in evidence. Some of the houses and inns were many centuries old. The University owned all the land thereabouts, and they did not countenance any of the tomfoolery called Progress. They wanted Cambridge left just as it was, a decision I would have to applaud wholeheartedly.

What a delight to rest in an ancient inn drinking the excellent light brown ale! While chatting convivially with the other customers, I exulted in a milieu of Jacobean tables and chairs, mullioned windows, exposed ceiling beams, rich dark oak wainscoting, an open-hearth stone fireplace, and finally church warden pipes on the wall, not added as a decorator's touch but centuries old and once used by the patrons of the inn – a jewel of a setting for one who needed no such encouragement to drink. Had this genteel place once been the favorite haunt of Edmund Spenser or John Milton? Had the youthful Wordsworth and his friend Coleridge sat in these very chairs quenching their thirsts from the lovely old pewter tankards? I did not know, but I did not doubt it, for this was a place of poets.

At the Red Cross in Cambridge, I got the name of an English family that entertained American fliers on weekends. Their name was Newman; and they lived in Royston, a town nearby. I was to spend many happy hours with them. Their home was a fine old Georgian mansion with lawn tennis courts, orchards, formal gardens, and beautiful groves of trees. These people were very kind to me. Each night my bed would be turned down. A glass of milk and a bowl of fruit were on the nightstand by my bed. Sometimes there would be a book of poetry or a magazine, too. They treated me like a son, and I shall never forget them.

See also Madingley.

CHICKSANDS PRIORY (*see Shefford*)

DIDDINGTON, HUNTINGDONSHIRE

Location: On the A1 just North of St Neots.
Comments: The first US hospital site in East Anglia to be turned over to the American forces in what was previously Diddington Place and a public park. The 49th Station Hospital opened for patients on 26 December 1942, staffed in its first months of operation by the US 2nd Evacuation Hospital, supplemented with Auxiliary Surgical Team personnel.

HAYNES CHURCH END, BEDFORDSHIRE

Location: Off the A6, heading N to Bedford. NNE of Clophill.
Comments: An attractive village with Elizabethan houses and traditional thatched cottages, it was the home of Sir George Carteret, the founder of New Jersey, who lived in Hawnes Hall (now Clarenden School).

HENLOW, BEDFORDSHIRE

Location: Just E of Shefford on the A6001 and A507.
Comments: Perhaps best known for RAF Henlow, first established in 1918 for the newly created Royal Flying Corps. The twelfth century church of St Mary the Virgin is in a beautiful setting on a rise with a village pump and horse trough. On the famous voyage of the *Mayflower* were John Tilley, his wife Joan and daughter Elizabeth, who were from Henlow parish. Through Reverend Ashford, a former vicar, links have been formed with the Pilgrim John Howland Society in Rhode Island. Their members have made pilgrimages to the church and have made generous donations, including a pewter spoon, a replica of the one carried on the *Mayflower*, which is now displayed in the church.

Islip, Northamptonshire

Description: Woolpack Inn.
Location: 6 Kettering Road, Islip, near Thrapston NN14 3JU (Tel: 01832 732578).
Comments: The sixteenth century inn was a traditional watering hole for wartime airmen stationed nearby. Islip, Long Island in New York was founded by the son of a Northamptonshire emigrant who became the first mayor of New York City in 1671.

King's Cliffe, Northamptonshire

Description: Fighter base used by the RAF, USAAF and Belgian units.
Location: 12 miles W of Peterborough, next to a Roman road off the A47 at Wansford and 1½ miles NE of King's Cliffe village.
Comments: Wartime home of the 20th Fighter Group of the 8th Air Force, which flew P-38H Lightnings and later P-51D Mustangs. An unusual memorial incorporating vertical representations of a Sptifire and Mustang wing 'to commemorate the eternal memory of those American, British, Belgian and Commonwealth airmen who gave their lives in the course of freedom 1943–45' is on the road from the village to Wansford. The memorial was unveiled on 10 December 1986.

Little Staughton, Bedfordshire

Description: Airfield made available to the 8th Air Force in 1942.
Location: Just N of Bushmead Priory W of Eaton Socon.
Comments: RAF airfield, later used by the 2nd Strategic Air Depot, which moved to Abbots Ripton in late 1943.

Madingley, Cambridgeshire

Description: Cambridge American Cemetery.
Location: Approximately 3 miles W of Cambridge on the A1303 road.
Comments: This imposing cemetery and memorial, which covers 30 acres, was constructed on behalf of the American

A funeral at Madingley cemetery in WW2. *(Vie Pete Worby)*

Battle Monuments Commission in 1956 and is dedicated to the lives of the US service personnel who perished whilst serving in the UK during World War II. At the entrance is the Visitors' Building and a flagpole 72 feet high, the base of which is inscribed with the quotation: 'to you from failing hands we threw the torch – be yours to hold it high' Running parallel with the A1303 are the Tablets of the Missing. A limestone wall extending 472 feet from the Visitors' Building to the Memorial Building is inscribed with the names of 5126 United States personnel who died or went missing on active service. At the western end of the wall is the Memorial Building, which is divided into a chapel and a museum showing the progress of the war between 1942 and 1945. The 3811 headstones in the cemetery are arranged in a fan of seven curved rows, all set within carefully maintained lawns. The cemetery is open daily between 8.00 am and 6.00 pm (April to September) and 8.00 am to 5.00 pm (October to March). Limited parking is available outside the main entrance. Tel: 01954 201350.

Madingley Cemetery, Cambridge. *(Author)*

MELCHBOURNE PARK (STATION 572), BEDFORDSHIRE

Description: 8th Air Force Ordnance Depot.
Location: Off the A6 N of Sharnbrook.
Comments: The Glenn Miller band played an open air concert here in front of the main house to 750 officers and EM on 21 July 1944.

MILTON ERNEST HALL (STATION 506), BEDFORDSHIRE

Description: HQ, 8th Air Force Service Command.
Location: On the A6 5 miles N of Bedford near Thurleigh and RAF Twinwoods airfields.
Comments: World famous for its association with bandleader Glenn Miller, whose band gave their first concert here on 8 July 1944 when a small group of musicians led by Sergeant Ray McKinley played at an officers' club dance. On 16 July the full band gave a concert in the grounds in front of 1600 officers and men and invited guests. Miller is reputed to have left the hall on 15 December for Twinwoods airfield nearby for a flight to Paris in a UC-64 Norseman, never to be seen again. After school one

Milton Ernest Hall. *(Richards)*

day Connie Richards, who used to obtain chewing gum by boiling two eggs hard and taking them to two Military Policemen on the gate at 8th Air Force HQ, Milton Ernest Hall, watched as two or three staff cars came out of the drive of the Hall.

> One contained The Andrew Sisters. We recognised them because we had seen them in a movie. In another car was Glenn Miller. One day Glenn Miller was playing at a dance to be held in the Club Castle there. I wanted to go so badly but my mum said 'No'. I had heard of Glenn Miller and liked his music in those days and to have a great band-leader in my village, I had to go, and that was that. So I arranged with my girlfriend who was going out with Staff Sergeant Max Calker, that they would get me in. That was justly done and that night I remember with pride seeing the band and I actually spoke to Glenn Miller. Broderick Crawford was there too. I would be glad when the war was over so I could get on with my life. We didn't get much food and clothes were rationed. At night my parents had to

put a blackout at the window so that no light showed
outside and we had to have evacuees from London to live
with us away from the bombs up there. We were quite
happy, we had to be. The months went by. I got to know a
lot of GIs and the village settled down to accepting them.
They were good to us then, as we were the 'Chewing Gum
Kids'. They learned to play skittles, darts, etc. There were
weddings at the Parish Church and film shows at the
school. The first one I went to was called 'Stage Door
Canteen'. Afterwards we had real ice cream. The
Americans took part in a lot of village functions and gave
so much to us. They were happy years, some tinged with
sadness. The guys from the 306th Bomb Group at
Thurleigh, about two miles from Milton Ernest, also went
to the pubs in the village. You asked, 'Where is Joe?' and
the answer you received was, 'Sorry honey, he didn't make
it back from today's mission'. I used to watch the B-17s go
out in the mornings and count them when they came back
later in the day. Around the Milton Ernest and Bedford
areas their memories still live.

NORTHAMPTON

Northampton played host to an estimated one million US
Service visitors during World War II. No fewer than 147,000
stayed at the Plough Hotel in Bridge Street, which also served as
the American Red Cross HQ and became known as the No. 1
American Leave Centre. The Stars and Stripes was raised over
the hotel each morning and lowered each sunset. The 92nd
Bomb Group diarist wrote of the town. 'In Northampton the
men went steadily to the Plough and the Angel, the Grand, the
Swan, the Black Boy, the Queen's Arms and came out less
steadily. The nightly liberty runs were loaded each way. The
cyclists and the thumbers continued to go to Wellingborough.
Billy Burke's Exchange Hotel drew a steady patronage; drawn
perhaps equally by Mr Burke's undeniable charm and his
woefully weak spirits.'

A US Servicemen's Centre, which arranged dances, baseball,
football and table tennis, was also located on the Market Square,

the site, too, of the *Chronicle* and *Echo* offices, which provided emergency sleeping accommodation for the men. Northampton's 'Friendship Committee', among many other functions and activities, hosted an All States Dinner at the Grand Hotel on 31 March 1944, sending invitations to a representative of each of the forty-eight states then comprising the Union. Allied Supreme Commander General Dwight D. Eisenhower wrote to Northampton to thank its people for their hospitality towards the Americans and his message was read out at a presentation in February 1945.

NORTHAMPTONSHIRE'S AMERICAN CONNECTIONS

George Washington's ancestry can be traced to the villages of Sulgrave, Great Brington, Thrapston and Islip. Sulgrave Manor, a perfect Shakespearean example of a small manor house and garden, was home of the forebears of 'the Father of his Country' for over 120 years.

The Church of St Mary the Virgin in Great Brington contains the tombs of Lawrence, the great-great-great grandfather of George Washington and Lawrence's brother Robert. The tombs date from the early 1600s. The Washington brothers came to the Bringtons from Sulgrave seeking employment on the estate of their cousins, the Spencers, family of the late Princess of Wales.

St James' Church in Thrapston is the site of a stone tablet bearing the arms of Sir John Washington, uncle to John Washington, George's great-grandfather who sailed to America in 1657. Sir John is buried somewhere in the churchyard. Montagu House, Sir John's house when he was Lord of the Manor of Thrapston, is located along Chancery Lane.

Josiah, the father of Benjamin Franklin, was born in the Northamptonshire village of Ecton, which was the Franklin family home for over 300 years. Josiah sailed to America in 1683 and Benjamin was born there twenty-three years later, the seventh child of his second wife. Various relics of the Franklins' presence in Ecton can still be seen, including the graves of Benjamin's aunt and uncle in the churchyard, a plaque in the Rectory commemorating his visit to the village in 1758 and the sites of the family's home and blacksmith's forge.

Lamport Hall was the seat of the Isham family for over 400 years. Chief among its descendants, were Thomas Jefferson and Robert E. Lee, who were distantly related through the Isham line.

Edmund and Judith Quincy travelled to America from the village of Achurch in 1633 and named the town of Quincy, Massachusetts. Tradition has it that ancestors of America's second presidential family, the Adams, originally came from the village of Flore. Members of the two families eventually married; one offspring was John Quincy Adams, sixth president of the United States.

The Garfields of Kilsby and Ashby St Ledgers were the fore-fathers of another president, James Garfield, whose tenure was one of the briefest in American history. His term was cut short by an assassin's bullet just a few months after his inauguration.

ODELL, BEDFORDSHIRE

Description: A pretty village with attractive limestone cottages and village pub on the green.
Location: On the Harrold Road S of Podington airfield.
Comments: Peter Buckley, America's earliest writer, was the rector of Odell's fifteenth century Church of All Saints for four-teen years. He was the founder of Concord, Massachusetts, where the first engagement of the War of Independence was later to take place. Buckley also published one of the first books in America. It was his library that helped establish that of the University of Harvard.

OLD WARDEN, BEDFORDSHIRE

Description: The Shuttleworth Collection, Old Warden Aerodrome, Biggleswade, Bedfordshire SG18 9EA.
Location: 2 miles W of the A1 where it bypasses Biggleswade.
Comments: This famous collection includes forty-seven examples of aircraft, historic vehicles, motorcycles, carriages and bicycles. The aircraft represent the progress of aviation from the Bleriot in 1909 to World War I fighters, the de Havilland sporting aeroplanes of the late 1920s and early 1930s,

along with the Hawker Hind and Gloster Gladiator of the late 1930s to the Spitfire of World War II fame. The collection is unique, as all the aircraft are airworthy, with about half being the sole surviving examples of their type. All are on view throughout the year in six hangars, with a selection of them flown from May to October, often with notable types from other collections. For further information, admission charges and group visit details telephone 01767 627288 or email collection@shuttleworth.org. The website address is www.shuttleworth.org. It is open all year round except Christmas week/New Year's Day. Air shows are on the first Sunday of each month from May to October. Evening air displays are held in June and August and the Sunset Flying Display in September. On flying days access to the collection is via the entrance in the village of Old Warden. Accommodation is available (Tel: 01767 –626200). Be sure to visit Cardington nearby (on a minor road south of the A603). The village is steeped in history associated with the R101 airship disaster of 1930 and the two massive airship sheds at the former Royal Airship Works at Cardington dominate the surrounding countryside. In World War II it was a Recruiting Centre.

OUNDLE, NORTHAMPTONSHIRE

Description: Historic town and a meeting place for many American airmen from the surrounding bases.
Location: On the A427/A605 in a loop of the River Nene.
Comments: One of the most attractive market towns in Northamptonshire and a popular watering hole for Americans based at King's Cliffe fighter base, Polebrook and Deenethorpe because of the large number of pubs and inns. The Tourist Information Office is at 14 West Street, Oundle, Peterborough PE8 4EF (Tel: 01832 274333).

SHEFFORD (CHICKSANDS PRIORY), BEDFORDSHIRE

Description: Military Communications Centre.
Location: Close to the village of Shefford.
Comments: This twelfth century Gilbertine Priory became home

to the Osborn family in 1576. Sir Danvers Osborn was appointed the governor of New York in 1753. His memory is commemorated by a town in Massachusetts named after him. Chicksands Priory is situated on what was RAF Chicksands, a base, which was home to part of the American Air Force from 1950. It was deactivated in 1995 and reactivated as HQ British Military Intelligence.

SPANHOE AIRFIELD, NORTHAMPTONSHIRE

Description: Base for the USAAF's 315th Troop Carrier Group of the 9th Air Force.
Location: Near Harringworth.
Comments: Dakota pilot Dick Kucklick flew the Glenn Miller Band to Orly outside Paris on 18 December 1944, after two days' postponement because of bad weather. Kucklick, 20 at the time, had been a devoted fan since his high school days in Northern Ohio. He was told before leaving England with his celebrity passengers that Major Miller had gone on ahead and would meet them at Orly. The official announcement of Glenn Miller's disappearance and presumed death, however, was not made until several days after the pilot returned to base.

TWINWOOD FARM, BEDFORDSHIRE

Description: RAF satellite airfield for Cranfield and 51 OTU (Operational Training Unit).
Location: Off the A6 3½ miles N of Bedford.
Comments: Legend has it that the famous bandleader Major Glenn Miller took off from the airfield on 15 December 1944 for Paris and was never seen again. However, no evidence or any tower flight log have ever been produced to prove that a UC-64 Norseman with Miller on board ever left the airfield on this date. Miller's AEF band had given a concert beside the control tower on 27 August 1944. The tower has been restored and is now a museum containing many items of Miller memorabilia. It is open at weekends from 10.30 am to 4.00 pm during the summer and closed throughout the winter. For further information about the museum contact Twinwood Events Ltd,

Twinwood Road, Clapham, Bedfordshire MK41 6AB. Tel: 01234-350413. Email: info@twinwoodevents.com Website: www.twinwoodevents.com

UPPER BENEFIELD, NORTHAMPTONSHIRE

Description: The Wheatsheaf Hotel, Upper Main Street, Upper Benefield, Peterborough PE8 5AN (Tel: 01832 205254).
Location: On the A427 W of Oundle and E of Weldon.
Comments: The haunt of many wartime American airmen, the hotel displays an impressive collection of memorabilia from the airfield at Deenthorpe, including a silk escape map, photographs and pieces from a B-17 crash and posters.

WELDON, NORTHAMPTONSHIRE

Description: The Church of St Mary the Virgin.
Location: On the A427 1 mile NE of Corby.

The stained glass window in memory of the 401st Bomb Group in the Church of St Mary the Virgin at Weldon. *(Author's Collection)*

Comments: There is a stained glass window in memory of the 401st Bomb Group in the church. The centre panels came from the base chapel and the side panels were presented and installed immediately after the war to commemorate the missions flown by the members of the USAAF 401st Bomb Group from the local airfield and to perpetuate the memory of those who did not return. The centre window depicts three B-17s flying above cloud in a darkening sky, a cross and jewelled crown and the inscription: 'Duty without hate. In memoriam, our comrades of the 401st Bombardment Group.' To the right are hands clasped in friendship beneath the Union Jack and the Stars and Stripes and to the left is a gold-winged '8' surmounted by the words '401st Bomber Group, 1943–1945, to Weldon Parish Church'. Below are the texts, 'He hath delivered my soul in peace from the battle that was against me' and below that, 'For there were many with me'. At the bottom of the central column, wound round a blunted sword, are the words, 'Duty Without Hate'. Also in the church is a treble bell donated by members of the 401st Bomb Group and their families in 1975 in memory of fallen comrades whose names are listed in a book in the tower. Keys are available from Rachel Webster (Tel: 01536 202317) and Edward Whitlam (Tel: 01536 265004).

WIMPOLE HALL, ARRINGTON NEAR ROYSTON HERTS SG8 0BW

Near Bassingbourn airfield is Wimpole Park, once the home of Rudyard Kipling, where the once proud avenue of elms pointing to the airfield was a natural recognition symbol for returning aircrews. It was here that the US 163rd General Hospital opened for patients in October 1944. Later, it became an assembly centre for patients from other hospitals being sent back to the ZOI. Tel: 01223 207801.

WOBURN ABBEY, BEDFORDSHIRE

Description: Family home of the Dukes of Bedford, which was used by the Political Warfare Executive in World War II.
Location: Off the M1 at Junction 13.

Comments: Standing in a beautifully landscaped 3000-acre Deer Park, the Abbey was originally built as a Cistercian Monastery in 1145 and was gifted to John, First Earl of Bedford, by Henry VIII after the dissolution of the monasteries. The Abbey contains an outstanding collection of early Tudor and Stuart portraits, and paintings by Van Dyck, Rembrandt, Canaletto and Reynolds, as well as an impressive array of English and French eighteenth and nineteenth century furniture, silverware and porcelain. In 1763 the Fourth Duke's son and heir founded the Bedfordshire militia, which saw service in America at the outbreak of the War of Independence and there were engaged in the defence of Baton Rouge and Savannah and Pensacola. (Tel: 01525 –290666). The Abbey is open every day from 28 March to 1 November. From 28 December to 23 March it is only open at weekends and bank holidays.

Appendix IV

Further Information

Bedford Tourist Information Centre

Bedford Tourist Information Centre,
10 St Paul's Square, Bedford MK40 1SL. Tel: 01234 215226.
Email: touristinfo@bedford.gov.uk
Website: www.bedford.gov.uk/tourism

East Northamptonshire Council

East Northamptonshire House, Cedar Drive, Thrapston,
Northamptonshire, NN14 4LZ. Tel: 01832 742000.
Website: www.east-northamptonshire.gov.uk

8th Air Force Historical Society

The 8th Air Force Historical Society is a US-based informal
organisation open to anyone interested in the history of the US
8th Air Force. The Society, which has 27,000 members, provides
information relating to the 8th Air Force, along with organising
visits for returning veterans. For more information contact: Mr
Gordon Richards, 8th Air Force Historical Society, The Croft, 26
Chapel Went Road, Haverhill, Suffolk, OB9 9SD. Tel: 01440
704014.

FRIENDS OF THE EIGHTH (FOTE)

Friends of the Eighth is a UK-based organisation that maintains a close liaison with the 8th Air Force Historical Society and with many US veterans' organisations. Assistance is rendered to veterans visiting the UK, either as individuals or in reunion parties. For further information contact: Mr Ron Mackay, 30 Whirlow Road, Crewe CW2 6SR. Tel: 01270 568723.

GLENN MILLER HISTORICAL SOCIETY

Contact Connie Richards: The Croft, 26 Chapel Went Road, Haverhill, Suffolk, OB9 9SD. Tel: 01440 704014

DUXFORD IMPERIAL WAR MUSEUM

A former 8th Air Force and RAF Fighter Station, now part of the Imperial War Museum, it features the finest collection of military and civil aircraft in Britain. Duxford's annual 'Flying Legends Air Display' every July is arguably the finest air show in the world. For further information contact: Imperial War Museum, Duxford Airfield, Cambridgeshire CB2 4QR. Tel: 01223 833000. The museum is open every day except from 24 to 26 December. In summer it is open from 10.00 am to 6.00 pm. From mid-March to mid-December it is open from 10.00 am to 4.00 pm.

Glossary

AD	Air Division
AEF	Allied Expeditionary Force
AFCC	Air Force Composite Command
FC	Fighter Command
FTR	Failed to Return
KIA	Killed in Action
MIA	Missing in Action
MPI	Mean Point of Impact
Point-blank Directive	The principle that the USAAF would bomb by day and the RAF at night.
SAD	Strategic Air Depot
SHAEF	Supreme Headquarters Allied Expeditionary Force
TDY	Temporary Duty
TFW	Tactical Fighter Wing
TRW	Tactical Reconnaissance Wing
USAAF	United States Army Air Force
USSTAF	Untied States Strategic Air Forces
ZOI	Zone of the Interior (USA)

Bibliography

Andrews, Paul M & Adams, William H., *Heavy Bombers of the Mighty Eighth* (Eighth Air Force Museum Foundation Project Bits & Pieces) 1995

Arbib Robert S. Jr, *Here We Are Together, The Notebook of an American Soldier in Britain*

Beaty David, *Light Perpetual: Aviators' Memorial Windows* (Airlife Publishing Ltd) 1995

Birdsall, Steve, *Pride of Seattle – The Story of the first 300 B-17Fs* (Squadron Signal) 1998

Birdsall, Steve & Freeman, Roger A. *Claims to Fame – The B-17 Flying Fortress* (Arms & Armour) 1994

Bishop, Cliff T., *Fortresses of the Big Triangle First* (East Anglia Books) 1986

Blakebrough, Ken, *The Fireball Outfit* (1968)

Bowden, Ray, *Plane Names & Fancy Noses – the 91st BG (H)* (Design Oracle Partnership) 1993

Bowman, Martin W., *Castles In The Air* (PSL) 1984 (Red Kite) 2001

Bowman, Martin W., *Flying To Glory* (PSL) 1992

Bowman, Martin W., *Echoes of East Anglia* (Halsgrove Publishing Ltd) 2006

Bowman, Martin W., *USAAF Handbook 1939–1945* (Sutton) 1997, 2003

Bowman, Martin W., *8th Air Force At War* (PSL) 1994

Bowman, Martin W., *Great American Air Battles* (Airlife Publishing Ltd) 1994

Bowman, Martin W., *The Bedford Triangle* (PSL) 1988, (Sutton) 1996, 2003

Bowman, Martin W., *Sentimental Journey* (Erskine Press) 2005

Bowman, Martin W., *Boeing B-17 Flying Fortress* (Crowood) 1998

Bowman, Martin W. *B-17 Groups of the Eighth Air Force in Focus* (Red Kite) 2004

Bowman, Martin W., *B-17 Flying Fortress Units of the Eighth Air Force (Part 1)* (Osprey) 2000

Bowman, Martin W., *Combat Legends B-17 Flying Fortress* (Airlife Publishing Ltd) 2002

Bowyer, Michael J. F., *Action Stations 1: East Anglia* (PSL) 1990

Congdon, Philip, *Behind the Hangar Doors* (Sonik)

Francis, Paul, *Military Airfield Architecture From Airships to the Jet Age* (PSL) 1996

Freeman, Roger A., *The Mighty Eighth* (MacDonald) 1970

Freeman, Roger A., *Airfields of the Eighth Then and Now* (After the Battle) 1978

Freeman, Roger A., *The Mighty Eighth in Colour* (Arms & Armour) 1991

Freeman, Roger A., *Mighty Eighth War Manual* (Jane's) 1984

Freeman, Roger A., *The Mighty Eighth In Art* (Arms & Armour) 1996

Freeman, Roger A., with Osborne, David, *The B-17 Flying Fortress Story* (Arms & Armour) 1998

Good Brown, James, *The Mighty Men of the 381st – Heroes All* (Publishers Press) 1984

Hale, Edwin R. W. and Turner, John Frayn, *The Yanks Are Coming* (Midas Books) 1983

Havelaar, Marion H. with Hess, William N., *The Ragged Irregulars of Bassingbourn* (Schiffer Military History) 1995

Innes, Graham Buchan, *British Airfield Buildings of the Second World War* (Midland) 1995

Innes, Graham Buchan, *British Airfield Buildings Expansion & Inter-War Periods* (Midland) 2000

Lande D. A., *From Somewhere in England* (Airlife Publishing Ltd) 1991

Lay, Beirne Jr and Bartlett, Sy, *Twelve O'Clock High* (Ballatine Books) 1948

Marriott, Leo, *British Military Airfields Then & Now* (Ian Allan Publishing) 1997

MacKay, Ron, *381st Bomb Group.* (Squadron Signal) 1994

McDowell, Ernest R., *Flying Fortress in Action* (Squadron Signal) 1987

Sloan, John S., *The Route as Briefed: The History of the 92nd Bombardment Group USAAF 1942–1945* (Argus Press Cleveland, Ohio) 1946

Smith Jnr, Ben, *Chick's Crew – A Tale of the Eighth Air Force* (Privately published) 1978

Smith David J., *Britain's Memorials & Mementoes* (PSL) 1992

Smith, John N., *Airfield Focus 37: Deenethorpe* (GMS) 1999

Smith, John N., *Airfield Focus 40: Molesworth* (GMS) 2000

Smith, John N., *Airfield Focus 50: Glatton/Conington* (GMS) 2002

Stapfer, Hans-Heiri, *Strangers In A Strange Land* (Squadron Signal) 1988

Strong, Russell A., *First Over Germany – A History of the 306th BG* (Hunter Publishing) 1982

Way, Chris, *Glenn Miller In Britain Then and Now* (After the Battle)